20 Iconic Items that Changed
the History of Style

a matter of
FASHION

FOREWORD

BY VALERIA MANFERTO DE FABIANIS

People usually think of fashion as an ephemeral, transient world: one season, a few days, and then one has to move on, in a continuous, incessant wheel of renewal. And while the latest spring "sensation" is being launched the winter collections are already being finished and one is planning ahead for the coming year.

Actually–and lately this has been increasingly evident–fashions often come around again, either as true "phenomena" (for example, in the case of vintage products) or as reinterpretations of classics.

Classics.

And here we come to the heart of the matter: not everything that is fashion passes. In fact there are creations that years after their appearance on the scene have maintained their capacity to represent elegance, style, and class.

This book presents twenty icons that summarize, in a few essential but unmatchable lines, the characteristics of the "designer label classic", created by great artists, legendary interpreters of fashion who have left their mark not only in their specific field, but in the very evolution of the conceptions of the times and of time itself.

One name will suffice here: Coco Chanel. She was an exceptional woman who tirelessly pursued progress and was often even well ahead of it. She marked the path toward great style with numerous, irreplaceable masterpieces of fashion. The brilliant portrait photographed by Boris Lipnitzki in 1936 captures some fundamentals of her genius: a "little black dress", a cascade of pearls, a perfume with an unmistakable character... and you can almost smell it.

Twenty milestones of fashion, all expressed in various shapes and colors. Some are exclusive articles, others are part of our everyday life. In short, to each his own for exclusive, refined elegance.

a Matter of FAShion

EDITED BY
**VALERIA MANFERTO
DE FABIANIS**

PREFACE
ALBERTA FERRETTI

TEXT
FEDERICO ROCCA

EDITORIAL COORDINATION **GIADA FRANCIA - GIORGIA RAINERI** GRAPHIC DESIGN **MARINELLA DEBERNARDI**

CONTENTS

PREFACE

BY ALBERTA FERRETTI

When I was asked to write the preface of this book I said yes, quite spontaneously, without thinking straight away about the question that I continued to ask myself for some days while observing the 20 cult objects, each of which corresponds to precise images, that are also symbolic and timeless. For example. I have always felt a strong attraction to jeans, which I have never worn but which I like a lot because they are a manifesto of liberty and independence. Essential as a novel by Hemingway, they have retained their rebellious overtones despite the huge, extraordinary success that has made them so popular across-the-board, without distinction among all social classes and age groups. The fact that jeans have a precise name–Levi's–leads them back to their origin and to a story that is so long and documented that each of us can call to mind photographs and scenes in movies in which Levi's share the leading role.

The icons of style presented in this book begin with this glorious example of equality and joie de vivre. They are objects and names that mirror the changes in our society and the birth of taste – objects that are quite different yet with a common denominator that is decisive in their creation: the slow and stratified elaboration of memory. Memory that means "re-seeing", "rethinking", "re-enjoying" "re-loving", "re-desiring." Much time is needed to elaborate an icon, and in fact none of the ones described in this book are recent, although they are all exceptionally contemporary. Think of Burberry, which developed progressively, much like a work of engineering, and which was commissioned to "serve and protect" the soldiers at the front, becoming the very emblem of the trench coat and of the English style–not only for men but also for women, who find a fascinating contrast to their femininity in its austere lines and "virility." This is also what happened to Lacoste, which was transformed into the polo shirt par excellence, armed with the strong recollection of that photograph that Henri Lartigue shot of René Lacoste, so agile and light on his feet that he seems to be moving as if blown by the wind.

The very expression of that period when Couture was born in Paris are those first French department stores that founded the major brands that to this day are irresistibly attractive, such as Louis Vuitton and Hermès, whose bags and scarves are authentic objects of desire.

I think that the Kelly and Birkin bags marked the very origin of the accessory phenomenon that had such a profound influence on the fashion of this decade and that brought about a true revolution. These bags may change their size, proportions and colors and still always be equal to themselves and marvelously up-to-date. Just like the mythical Chanel 2.55, the ambassador of the Chanel style in perfume and tailleurs.

Indisputably current like the little black dress, are the Gucci Jackie Bag, Ray-Ban and Persol as well as Moncler, which marked one of the greatest changes in the history of clothing, bringing to the cities the comfort and protection of mountaineering.

I would like to conclude my thoughts by dwelling on shoes: the All Stars, in their openly declared athleticism, or

the perfection of Manolo Blahnik's stiletto, represent two different viewpoints on seduction and femininity. Not two opposed ideologies, but certainly two different aesthetics. And who can ever forget the ballerina pumps and the image of Audrey Hepburn with her light step, so natural and self-assured?

So why have these objects become true icons of style? Perhaps it's because they were created in a period when, unlike the present, every project was planned from beginning to end and was not subject to the pressure of contemporary rhythm, so burdened with messages and expectations. Perhaps because they were created in a natural way, without exaggerated or pretentious ambitions, and had a specific use and a specific purpose. Perhaps, and above all, because they were able to capture and reflect the spirit of society, revealing its changes and following its evolution in time and beyond.

WHAT IS ESSENTIAL IN FASHION

Essential Fashion? It's all very well saying "essential", but what does "essential" mean? What can be placed under the heading of this adjective that is used and abused so much and at the same time is so vague? A reliable dictionary may help clear up any doubts. Collins English Dictionary gives the following meanings:

ESSENTIAL, adj.
1) vitally important; absolutely necessary
2) basic; fundamental → the essential feature
3) completely realized; absolute; perfect → essential beauty
4) (biochemistry) (of an amino acid or a fatty acid) necessary for the normal growth of an organism but not synthesized by the organism and therefore required in the diet
5) derived from or relating to an extract of a plant, drug, etc. → an essential oil
6) (logic) (of a property) guaranteed by the identity of the subject; necessary. Thus, if having the atomic number 79 is an essential property of gold, nothing can be gold unless it has that atomic number
7) (music) denoting or relating to a note that belongs to the fundamental harmony of a chord or piece
8) (pathology) (of a disease) having no obvious external cause → essential hypertension
9) (geology) (of a mineral constituent of a rock) necessary for defining the classification of a rock. Its absence alters the rock's name and classification

Our aim is to define "essential fashion", that is, to select, from the history of couture, those fashion "items" that have the right and, the obligation, to appear in this volume. Consequently, we can safely omit interpretations 4-9 in the Collins set above and concentrate on the other more generic ones.

As for the fact that a dress or a shoe could be "vitally important, absolutely necessary"… well, it might be quite difficult to persuade a woman that the contrary is true. However, in order to be realistic, or at least objective, we must admit that one could live (perhaps not well) without a designer handbag or a pair of trendy shoes. In short, survival is not a subject one brings up when discussing fashion, especially these days when the serious economic crisis makes basic goods even more indispensable.

More appropriate, if well interpreted, is the concept of "basic, fundamental." Because, in effect, the twenty "items" (let's use that name, the most neutral and generic form available) whose history and curious aspects are discussed in this volume, represent, to a certain degree, the very "quintessence" of fashion–or perhaps we should say of clothing and accessories–in the 20th-century (although, as we shall see, many of these "items" go much farther back in time). They represent the fundamental stages, the turning points, the inevitable cross-roads–much like those games in which, by connecting the dots, you create a drawing that makes sense out of something that was only vaguely perceivable beforehand. Similarly, the twenty "items" described in this book are like those dots whose totality follows a pre-established logic and path that corresponds to a complex drawing that could represent any one of the many stories of fashion.

This appropriate definition is accompanied by another complementary one. Apart from the "fundamental" points of the history of fashion we also want to describe those that are "totally realized" and "perfect." Whether born in a state of grace, or having evolved, through a series of natural developments and transformations, to a state of "impeccable completeness", the substance does not change: whatever is "essential" is a perfect specimen of its kind and could not be better. Let's consider jeans: are there any other pants that are more practical and versatile, and at the same time so sexy? Absolutely not. Or take the Chanel 2.55, the Hermès Birkin and Kelly bags, or the Gucci Jackie bag. Can anyone imagine handbags more impeccable and complete, despite their apparent simplicity, handbags closer to the "ideal" of a universal handbag? The answer is the same: absolutely not.

In short, "essential" is a kind of synthesis of the concepts expressed by two other definitions so much used and abused used in fashion journalist lingo: "must-have" and "evergreen." Essential is that which one must potentially have in order to be "in" but is not connected to the circumstances of the moment; rather, it is elevated, as much as possible, to the temporal parameters of eternity. Having established the criteria for fashion items to be classified as "essential", there remains only the cruel game of which are to be included. As is the case with all choices here too rigor and logic may very well be augmented by discretion. This book will deal with only twenty "essential items", because we have established that boundary. It is obvious that, despite everything, personal taste and sensitivity also play a role in the process of selection, as well as more vague criteria such as curiosity and, wherever possible, originality. Taking a glance at the list of items that "haven't made it", what comes to mind is that a second volume might already be predictable. Is the tuxedo (*le smoking*) designed by Yves Saint Laurent perhaps any less essential than the Moncler duvet? Is a white shirt less essential than the French sailor shirt? Is the miniskirt less essential than the Chanel tailleur, or the deconstructed Armani jacket less essential than the Burberry trench coat? And the same can be said for the Max Mara camel hair overcoat, combat boots, studded leather jackets, etc. Thus, it is a question of choice, and as such is open to discussion but certainly coherent, considering the aims of this book. But it must be said that a certain dose of underlying heterogeneity apparently makes the selection of the twenty items somewhat "loose." In the first place, these items are not only items of clothing, since we know what powerful fascination and attraction accessories can have. And there is also perfume, because Chanel N°5 seems no less essential and no less an integral part of fashion, so that including it in our list seemed imperative.

Some of the items are closely connected to a designer label, while others are not. The square foulard par excellence is the one designed by Hermès, just as the word trench coat is commonly associated with Burberry. But while jeans were "born" as Levi's, they became so popular and widespread that they now belong to everybody. And the same holds true for the most iconic item considered here: the little black dress (LBD). The black sheath dress was created by Coco Chanel and was "improved" by Hubert de Givenchy, but it was then transformed into such an abstract concept that it lent itself, fortunately, to the interpretation of any designer label or stylist.

Some of the items are considered to be the pinnacle of class and elegance, while others are the very essence of casual style. From the Chanel bouclé tailleur to Converse sneakers, the entire range of occasions seems to be represented. And rightly so.

Not all the selected items are exclusively for women; in fact, many have been "purloined" from men's wear in the game of role-reversal so delightfully typical of contemporary fashion. But this too is a consequence of the large number and variety of the origins of these items. Many of those selected here were created in spheres that are distant, if not diametrically opposed, to those of conventional fashion. For example, sports stadiums, ski runs, war trenches, mines, and even streets have been (and continue to be) the "birthplaces" of iconic and essential items in contemporary fashion. This phenomenon has even shed light on one of the most paradoxical boundaries of the fashion "system": with rare exceptions it is unable to produce true must-haves that are programmed as such beforehand in keeping with a specific plan. Indeed, one might go so far as to say that the only stylist who really succeeded in creating items with the conscious aim of making them become legendary, was Coco Chanel, who is considered the greatest stylist of all.

But if it seems that the iconic items in this volume are distinguished by so many different features, there are many more features that confer a basically homogeneous character to the group.

As we saw above, the items described were not created with the aim of being must-haves, as their production was often a case of pure chance. Random events or meetings, fortuitous circumstances, and coincidences triggered the creation of an icon. What was the most sensational instance of this phenomenon? The Hermès Birkin handbag, which was born thanks to a casual meeting, on an airplane, of a chief executive of a luxury goods manufacturer and a sophisticated actress. There was no premeditation or design here, only pure and perfect happenstance.

The second common feature of all the items is that each has a history, often with epic overtones, and in any case always adventurous. Having a past to relate, a tradition to display, a heritage to boast, is a common thread that subtly links everything that has an "essential" appeal in fasion – especially at this historic moment, when a prestigious background is perceived as added value, particularly in those countries that have only recently become curious about and receptive to the world of fashion and its dynamics. Thus, almost all the items in this volume were created in the distant past thanks to the acumen, intuition and curiosity of a single, gifted person who was either the founder or member of a fashion dynasty, the protagonist of one chapter of the "minor" saga of an industry that is interwoven with the "great" history of humanity.

Another common denominator among the twenty items is that each was created for practical rather than aesthetic reasons. And if that statement can be immediately and obviously recognized as valid as, for example, in the case of Louis Vuitton luggage, it may come as a surprise that, when all is said and done, the same holds true for the more "charming" accessories like Chanel 2.55 or for such specimens of contemporary *bon ton* as the Chanel tailleur or the Repetto ballerina shoes. So a common bond might be the following: what is essential is beautiful, but an item is beautiful if its shape and aesthetics are justified by a specific, "concrete" use or function. And then there is the matter of popularity. All the legendary items presented in this book made their sensational entrance into the collective imagination and remained there–in both the popular sphere as well as the more sophisticated (and snobbish, if you wish) one of the initiated. Transcending the narrow and useless circles of fashion in the strict sense of the word, the "magnificent twenty" have permeated popular culture through a one-to-one exchange that has allowed mass culture to "violate" them by desacralizing them while at the same time, paradoxically, elevating them to a higher rank. It is quite easy, even inevitable, to associate each of them with the well-known, world-famous face of a star, usually a movie star. The Kelly handbag, obviously, cannot be separated from the mythical image of Princess Grace, after whom it was named, and jeans cannot but evoke the images of James Dean and Marlon Brando – just as Ray-Ban sunglasses go hand in hand with the Blues Brothers and the little black dress with Audrey Hepburn. Ballerinas call to mind, in a flash, the pouting Brigitte Bardot, while the name Manolo Blahnik is bound to be linked to the fictional character Carrie Bradshaw as interpreted by Sarah Jessica Parker. And so forth.

Finally, there is flexibility, which may be the most conspicuous and indispensable common feature among all the twenty evergreen items of Essential Fashion. They have all passed through the turbulent course of capricious fashions and trends unscathed, and emerged even stronger. They have all survived the fickle seasons and styles that, like a perpetual merry-go-round, have animated the world of fashion, making it appear to be elusive and impalpable. All of them have succeeded in adapting to changing tastes, which frequently becomes antithetical. To varying degrees, all have manifested versatility and elasticity, which have been key to their survival as well as to their indomitable and universal success. They are part of the fashion world but remain outside it a little, in order to dominate and not be dominated, in order to be points of reference and not victims to be pulverized by its mechanism.

This is so because the twenty icons of Essential Fashion tell us a lot about the men and women who choose to wear them. And to a certain degree they also help those men and women understand and express something about themselves, something that is different in everyone. It could not be otherwise.

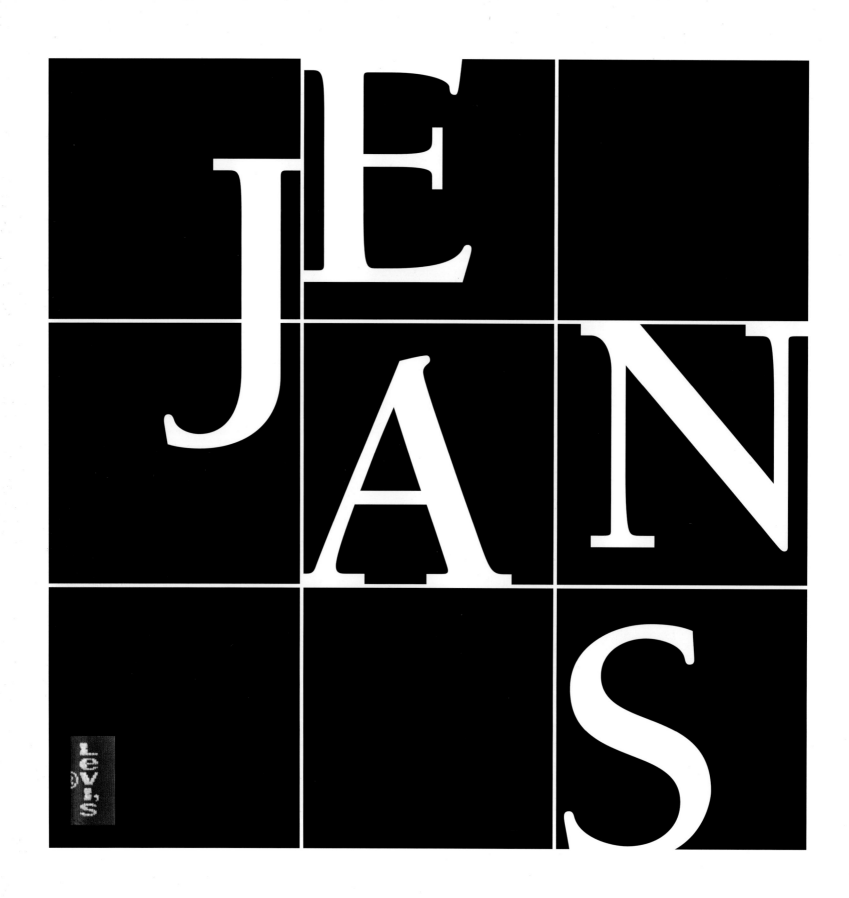

Levi's. From mines to catwalks.

*P*robably nothing like jeans has mirrored so precisely and faithfully the profound changes that have revolutionized Western society in the 20th-century. Perhaps they were not the mainspring that triggered these changes, because after all they are nothing more than a pair of pants, but if it is true that, as philosopher Jean Baudrillard wrote, "the world changes but jeans do not", it is also true that these irrepressible blue pants have witnessed all the transformations of our contemporary world.

And this all began, strange to say, with the least revolutionary thing one could imagine, a bureaucratic document. On 20 May 1873 Jacob Davis and Levi Strauss received, from the U.S. Patent and Trademark Office, U.S. patent no. 139,121 for their original method of strengthening the rough canvas work pants (which were then called "waist overalls") by inserting copper rivets into the fabric. Thus, a stamped document gave rise to a myth of modern fashion, which Diana Vreeland defined with surreal humor as "the most beautiful things since the gondola."

Jacob Davis, born in 1834 in Riga, Latvia, was a tailor from Reno, Nevada, with a wandering history and many past failures – that is until a minor invention, and above all the idea of having it patented, changed his life. While making a pair of work pants for a difficult client he decided to put some small metal studs on the pockets to prevent them from tearing. But he did not have the 68 dollars needed to patent his process and so decided to try to persuade someone he knew to become his partner: Levi Strauss, a Jewish immigrant, like himself, from whom he regularly bought de Nîmes cloth (which became "denim" in English) which he used to make his work pants.

Levi Strauss was born in Buttenheim, Bavaria in 1829. In 1847 he went to New York, where his older brothers Jonas and Louis had a dry-goods business. He then moved to Louisville, Kentucky where he worked with his uncle Daniel Goldman for five years, after which he felt the urge to go to California, where gold had been discovered and it was said that one could get rich quickly. But it was not gold that interested him; it was those who sought gold, the prospectors. In 1853 he was in San Francisco, where he founded the Levi Strauss dry-goods wholesale establishment, which sold buttons, underwear, handkerchiefs and above all tough canvas cloth that was used to make sails and was also bought by the desperate (or courageous) prospectors to cover their Conestoga wagons. From 1848 to 1855 over 300,000 people went

17 A US Navy sailor coping with his laundry in 1942.

It was time for young people to change the world, and conquer their space to the sound of a rock & roll beat.

West, and this was a big potential market for the enterprising Strauss. Among the best-selling items in Strauss's highly successful store were the practical, loose-fitting pants–at first made of canvas and then of denim–that gold miners wore over their normal clothing, durable and with pockets that did not rip, where they could safely put their work tools or, in the case of the rare lucky ones, their gold nuggets.

Davis's invention was nothing more or less than a technical improvement on workwear that was already popular. However, the waist overalls patented by Davis and Strauss had the advantage of codifying what, in the 1950s, were known as blue jeans which, despite undergoing a series of changes and variations, are basically the same as they were in 1873.

Levi Strauss made his fortune with miners, but not only with miners. It was when gold began to run out and the gold rush declined, and the many laborers, working for the railroads, purchased the highly durable pants (wearing them over their street clothes) that Strauss began to manufacture on an industrial scale and sell at a low price of $1.25. Strauss soon became a millionaire. After the laborers, the next wave of buyers consisted of farmers, and then cowboys, who could be seen in the boundless prairies as well as in movies ranging from the wobbly *Great Train Robbery* (1903) to the legendary *Stagecoach* (1939), starring John Wayne. Jeans were purchased by the US Navy, whose sailors wore them while fighting in World War II. Even when the famous patent expired in 1890, thus paving the way for competitors, the company's turnover increased. A few decades later Wrangler also began to make jeans. But there was more than enough business for everyone.

What led jeans to worldwide fame in the 1950s, however, were the masses of young Americans who wore them. But there was trouble in store for anyone who dared called them "uniforms", because paradoxically, there was nothing more impervious to standardization than jeans. The time was ripe for a revolution, a revolution in fashion and custom. The false myths of the bigots and bourgeoisie of the preceding generation were now out of fashion and were about to be sacrificed on the altar of society. It was time for young people to change the world, kick the shins of the hypocrisy of conformism, and conquer their space to the sound of a rock & roll beat. Their gurus were movie icons who, with a sad, sensual and intransigent look, and a pair of jeans, were able to change the world. These were the "bad boys" with whom the young generation identified, those who embodied its healthy but unconscious ideals: Marlon Brando, James Dean and Elvis Presley. The first, immortalized in László Benedek's *The Wild One* (1953), with his black leather Perfecto jacket, white T-shirt and pouting lips, paved the way, on his Triumph Thunderbird 6T motorcycle, for the fragile and vulnerable rebels in jeans who would later invade cities and small towns

19 With pouting lips, black leather Perfecto jacket, white T-Shirt, and jeans: Marlon Brando, star of *The Wild One* (1953) is revived in this 1980s Levi ad.

across the United States. Then there was James Dean, emblem of that *Rebel Without a Cause* (1955), who shattered conventions and inveighed against the status quo. His was a wholly inner, personal rebellion, which then erupted into a collective one orchestrated by organized, politically aware movements. Then there was Elvis Presley, who represented a lighter and more playful side of this rebellion, using songs, brilliantined curls that defied gravity, and uninhibited grinding. On the one hand, jeans were the picklock of anti-conformism used to unhinge the established rules, and on the other were an intolerable affront to morality, judging from the letters of outrage and protest that respectable housewives wrote to the Levi Strauss company, which in a 1957 ad showed a boy in jeans under the slogan "Right for School."

George Bernard Shaw once wrote that "a fashion is nothing but an induced epidemic." Just like a virus that strikes the younger strata of society, "jeans mania" spread across the United States. In 1958, one newspaper wrote that around 90% of young Americans wore them everywhere except in bed and in church. The "invasion" of Europe was inevitable and rapid, as was their popularity in the rest of the world. And there was no gender distinction either, because jeans were the first truly unisex fashion item in history. Decade after decade, changes were made in the washing and finishing processes and in the wearability, but jeans retained the same transgressive and revolutionary impact and impetus.

The transition from the ingenuousness of anti-fashion to the rules of Fashion was fatal: in the 1980s jeans were devoured voraciously and as a result some of their iconoclastic impact was attenuated on the catwalks of leading designer labels and stylists. But only up to a certain point. Because, like glowing embers, the two billion pairs of jeans sold every year throughout the world have maintained their subversive force intact, even if at times it may appear to be latent. Is that due to their color–always blue? Perhaps. Because, as Baudrillard wrote, blue has undoubtedly counted a lot in the worldwide success of jeans, not only as a symbolic color but also as a "utopian" color. Certainly, jeans have been manufactured in all colors but we know very well that all the others are inappropriate variations. All in all, the special color blue is the only one that makes you dream: the color of the sky, of eternity, yet light and lacking in demands.

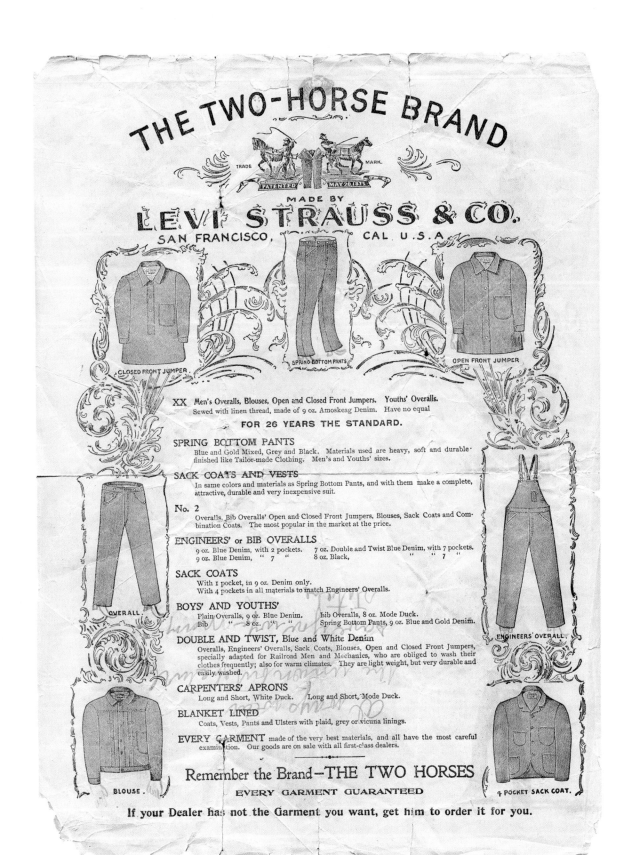

20 and 21 The Levi models in their early stores (right) and in early 20th-century
ads (above) evoked their origin as workwear, but their transformation into a casual
fashion icon was just around the corner.

BLUE JEANS

22-23 During World War II, American women did not stand idly by; on the contrary, jeans became the uniform of the army of women workers.

*Like a virus, "jeans mania"
spread across the Unites States.*

24 and 25 James Dean in *Giant* (1956) and in
a 1980s ad promoting jeans designed for women.

They are the most popular pants in the world and yet embody a spirit of rebellion.

26 Western hero John Wayne, with his son, on the set of *The War Wagon* (1967).

27 The unmistakable silhouette of the "Boss", Bruce Springsteen, in 1985.

LOUIS VUITTON

Style "on the road."

There are meetings–sometimes chance and insignificant–that can change one's very existence. One such meeting happened to Louis Vuitton and it leads us to a question with philosophical overtones: if that propitious meeting had not taken place, would the destiny of the French craftsman really have been so different, and would he have gained the success that to this day, around 150 years later, has been enjoyed by one of the leading luxury brands in the world?

Louis Vuitton was born in 1821 in Anchay, a small village in the Jura region of France. His father was a farmer and his mother a milliner. She died when Louis was only ten years old and, as in a fairy tale, his stepmother was not terribly fond of her stepchild, to say the least, so Louis decided to run away from home and seek his fortune. He went on foot to Paris, where he finally arrived almost 300 miles and more than two years later. In Paris he was certainly not an idler; on the contrary, he soon found a job as an errand boy and apprentice for a well-known luggage-maker, Monsieur Maréchal. At that time luggage-making was much more profitable and important that we might imagine today. It did not merely consist of making and selling luggage and trunks, but rather of packing clothing and personal belongings for members of the upper middle class and aristocracy, who were beginning to take more and more long trips, both by sea and land, during which they felt the need to carry with them everything they considered indispensable (as well as many superfluous belongings) in order to enjoy their normal existence of comfort and luxury while they were abroad.

Louis Vuitton gained valuable experience and expertise as a "packer" and began to frequent so-called Parisian high society, acquiring a certain notoriety in his field. And this would probably have been his simple and dignified lot had he not crossed paths–the chance meeting mentioned earlier–with Eugénie de Montijo, wife of the French emperor Napoleon III, a woman who was not only very powerful but also an extremely vain follower of fashion, so much so that she was considered one of the most elegant (if not the most elegant) women of her time. The empress is to be credited, above all, with having brought about the rise and fame of Charles Frederick Worth, her favorite tailor, considered to be the father of modern haute couture. Wearing her tailor's splendid clothes and adorned with fabulous jewels,

33 The photograph that immortalized model Linda Harper in the mid-1950s - a blend of irony and glamor.

By observing the limitations of luggage then being used, Vuitton understood how to create luggage for the future.

Eugénie had several portraits painted by the artist Franz Xaver Winterhalter. But she is also to be credited with having introduced the young Vuitton, who was working for her at the Tuileries and during her many trips, to the noblewomen who frequented her husband's court, the nerve center of imperial luxury and pomp, the melting pot of the crème de la crème of French high society. This paved the way for his future success; thanks to the empress, Vuitton became number one in his field. Yet fame did not seem to be enough for him. Vuitton was not the type of person who was easily satisfied.

And in 1854 he found the courage to follow his instinct and set up in business, opening his first luggage store in the Rue Neuves-des-Capucines. The workshop sign was an honest declaration of his aims: "Securely packs the most fragile objects. Specializing in packing fashions." The instinct that led to his great success was simple yet acute. Less than twenty years earlier the first French railway line, the Paris Saint-Germain, had been built, and the first transatlantic voyages were being made with steampowered or propeller-driven ships. The world of travel was rapidly evolving, but cumbersome luggage that faithfully followed its owner had not developed to keep pace. The old trunks had rounded tops and could not be stacked. Furthermore, being made of leather they were not adequately resistant to water, humidity and bad weather in general. Louis Vuitton came up with the idea of his life. By simply observing the limitations of luggage then in use, he conceived how to improve it for the future. In 1858 he made his first trunk, a perfect parallelepiped made of poplar wood and gray canvas that, at the outset, became the hallmark of his company. The new trunk was waterproof, light, stackable, and marked the birth of modern luggage. Louis Vuitton's fundamental technical brainchild was followed by another that was no less fundamental to the success of his company.

He understood that every client had different needs. Consequently, "customize" soon became his byword; his new mission was to offer his clients exactly what each of them wanted. Precisely because of this flexibility and versatility he received personal orders from clients as demanding as they were im-

34 This late 19th-century hatbox, for a top hat, is just one example of a vast range that Vuitton offered to travelers of the time.

35 Two early 20th-century monogramed canvas suitcases: vintage yet stylishly modern.

portant: from Ismail Pasha, the viceroy of Egypt, who used Vuitton trunks during his trip to the inauguration of the Suez Canal; from Grand Duke Nicholas, the future czar of Russia; from King Alfonso XII of Spain; and from explorer Savorgnan de Brazza, who asked Vuitton to make him a foldable trunk that, when opened, became a camp bed on which he could rest during his expedition to discover the source of the Congo River.

From that time to the present there has been a continuous course toward the definition of modern "travel luxury", a series of stages that have codified what today is universally known as the Louis Vuitton style. In 1872 the company decided to introduce a new canvas trunk with beige and red stripes and in 1875 they launched the vertical Wardrobe trunk, complete with hangers and drawers. The following year Georges, Louis's son, created the five-tumbler lock system, proclaimed as "Houdini-proof." The year 1888 witnessed the birth of the iconic Damier checkerboard pattern, while the equally famous (and imitated) Monogram came out only eight years later. The invention of the automobile triggered the creation of the first small, soft suitcases that could be transported easily even on these new, "high-speed contraptions": from the Steamer Bag to the Keepall and the legendary and ageless Speedy and Noé (Noah) models. With time, the list of faithful and famous clients became longer and longer: Coco Chanel, the Aga Khan, the Vanderbilts, Charles Lindbergh and the soprano Lily Pons, who could not do without her 36 pairs of shoes wherever she went. But perhaps it is the movie stars, assaulted by the paparazzi in airports all over the world, who can best attest to the popularity of Vuitton luxury leather goods. Mary Pickford, Marlene Dietrich, Lauren Bacall, Cary Grant and, today, Sharon Stone–to mention but a few of the most famous–never traveled (or travel) without their set of Vuitton suitcases. These suitcases sometimes even steal the scene and enjoy their own celebrity and acclaim. In fact, is it the luggage or the actors (Owen Wilson, Adrien Brody, and Jason Schwartzman) who star in Wes Anderson's cult movie *The Darjeeling Limited* (2007)?

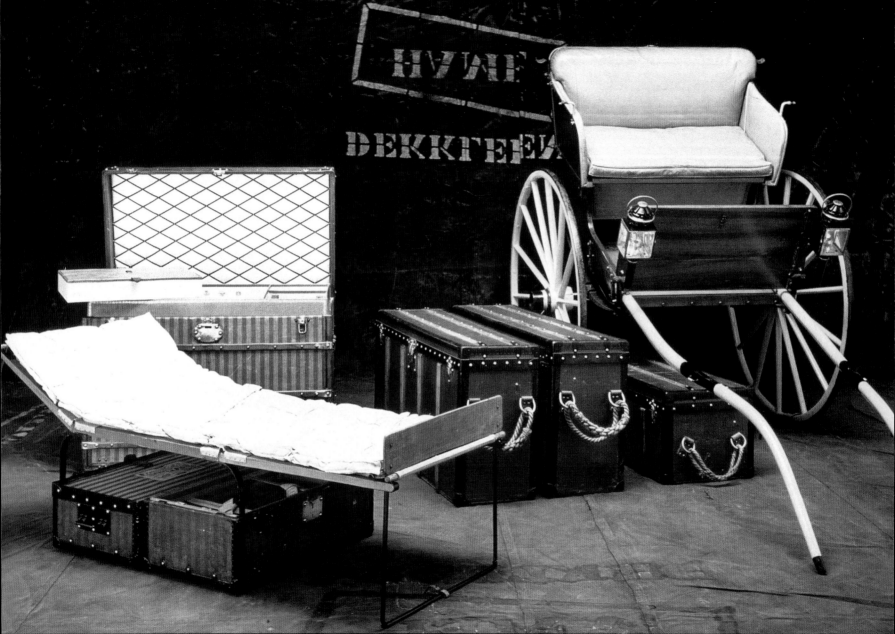

Fulfilling his clients' every need became Louis Vuitton's mission.

38 Over the years, the range of Vuitton products has included chests of drawers and foldaway writing desks
so that clients could travel with the same elegance and style they enjoyed in their everyday life.

39 "I love Vuitton luggage. It is elegant and practical," said actress Jermaine Clussey, who took part in the firm's
testimonial ad campaign.

Some journeys cannot be put into

40-41 Keith Richards, portrayed in 2008 by Annie Leibovitz, is one famous fan who has lent his image to the brand. Others over the years have included Angelina Jolie, Sean Connery, U2's Bono and Mikhail Gorbachev.

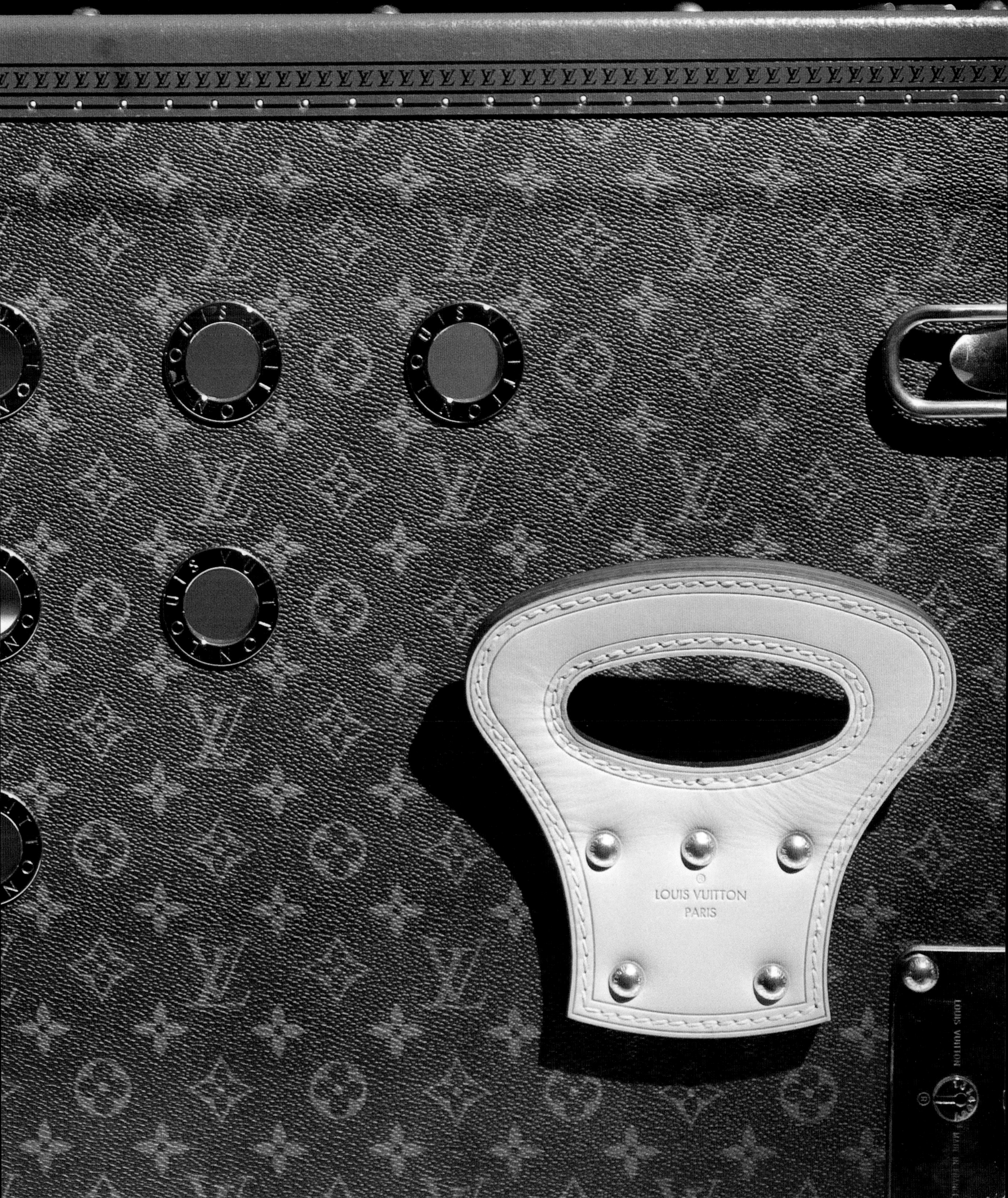
LOUIS VUITTON
PARIS

the TrE NchCoaT

Burberry. The perfect "British style."

BURBERRY

The classic trench coat–whether worn by distinguished gentlemen, pop stars off stage, urban dark ladies trying to lend an air of mystery to their persona, or TV detectives–seems to be immutable and in a certain sense "predictable" and "inevitable", like a fact or a dogma. Something that exists and has probably always existed, something that does not need to be questioned. We no longer wonder about the reasons behind its special, unique features, and its details no longer arouse our curiosity as they once did. The D-rings hanging from the belt; the shoulder and cuff straps; the storm flap; the raglan sleeves; the overlapping fabric on the most exposed parts such as the chest; and the V-neck and metal hooks and eyes on the collar. It is hard to think that all this was created for purely aesthetic reasons. Of course, a trench coat would not have the same fascination if even one of the above elements were missing, but there must be something more than meets the eye, after all. Like the tailbone, which is there in the human skeleton and seems no longer to serve any purpose. But this relic of an ancient appendage tells us quite a lot about what our ancestors were like and how they might have used a tail.

Thus, we can imagine hand grenades, or even less offensive equipment such as maps or small knives, hanging from the D rings. We suppose that epaulets and insignia of rank could be attached to the shoulder straps. The storm flaps or shields could be closed so that the coat was almost like a sort of diving suit that was virtually weather-proof. And by itself the overlap clearly indicates its insulating properties. A critical eye and some intuition suffice to discern, in those highly "transparent" signs, the origins of this coat, which was created as military clothing. For that matter its provenance is made clear by its very name, which refers to trench warfare.

The person who invented the trench coat was Englishman Thomas Burberry. He was a draper's apprentice who in 1856, at the age of twenty-one, decided to open his first outlet shop in Basingstoke, Hampshire. He suffered from rheumatism and, naturally, the damp British climate aggravated his condition. So, although we may call it self-interest, the fact remains that Burberry did his utmost to create clothing that would protect people from cold and damp while at the same be light-

45 Top model Kate Moss in an ad campaign for Burberry, of which she is a devotee and faithful icon.
47 The unmistakable tartan pattern against a beige background is the true signature of the Burberry brand.

weight and comfortable. And in 1870 the new coat became the pride and joy of his company: his research led him to produce and sell mantles and overcoats that immediately became popular among hunters and sportsmen. Not satisfied with this, in 1880 he invented–and patented eight years later–a radically innovative cloth that would make him a fortune: gabardine. In truth, other people had devised various technical methods to waterproof fabric, one of whom was Scotsman Charles Macintosh, who by 1823 had applied a solution of rubber dissolved by naphtha between two layers of wool that made the fabric resistant to the light rain so common in Britain. But the great advantage of Burberry's invention was that it was light and breathable like cotton; what is more, it did not have the unpleasant smell of rubber. Burberry's secret lay in his waterproofing the yarn before it was woven, and also in the fact that the warp and weft of the yarn had a diagonal pattern which threw off raindrops.

1895 marked the official birth of the Tielocken–this was the name of the forerunner of the trench coat–made of gabardine, which in a short time became Burberry's bestselling line at its first outlet in London's Haymarket. Success was confirmed by the overcoat being used by British forces during the Second Boer War in South Africa (1899-1902). If, in 1911, the first person to reach the South Pole, Captain Roald Amundsen, wore clothing and camped in tents made by Burberry, this means that one could rely on the performance of the raincoat. At the outbreak of World War I the War Ministry once again asked Burberry to produce overcoats for the officers at the front. The Tielocken underwent a few minor alterations and became the legendary trench coat, exactly the same one we all know and wear today, fortunately far from the muddy trenches.

Many of the 500,000 trench coats that were sent to the front between 1914 and 1918 returned home intact. Like the one belonging to an RAF officer who wrote the following grateful letter to the Burberry company: "During the war I crashed in the English Channel while wearing a Burberry trench coat. I had to abandon it. It was brought back to me a week later, and despite the fact that it had been in the water for five days I wore it again and it is still in perfect shape." Not bad publicity, to be sure. At least as persuasive as the involuntary tributes made by Captain John Alcock and Lieutenant

Arthur Whitten Brown, who wore Burberry trench coats during one of the most epoch-making feats in the postwar period, the first non-stop flight across the Atlantic, in 1919. Seventy-two hours at the mercy of the elements is quite an achievement, for men or raincoats.

In short, the trench coat became synonymous with heroism. Male movie stars began to wear it when playing the role of tough, poker-faced detectives in black-and-white films, while female leads managed to exude sensuality when wrapped in a trench coat: a case of the tried and true recipe of a drop of masculinity in a glass of femininity, which proved to be an explosive mixture. By the 1920s even civilians began to fall in love with the trench coat. In order to comply with their aesthetic needs and tastes, Burberry began to line the inside of the trench coat with the famous checkerboard pattern, the Nova Scotia tartan.

While at the front, during World War II, the trench coat gave way to more practical, shorter overcoats. Back in British cities the trench coat became a staple and a stereotype on a par with umbrellas, derby hats, double-decker buses and red telephone boxes. To this day the Burberry trench coat is a sort of calling card of Britishness, so much so that Her Majesty Queen Elizabeth II and the Prince of Wales conferred royal warrants of appointment on the company in 1955 and 1989.

The number of pieces of cloth that go into making a trench coat has always been the same – twenty-six – and the double-breasted section has always had ten buttons. Yet this iconic item has grown, matured and met increasingly sophisticated public needs, especially in recent years, thanks to the intelligence and insight of Christopher Bailey, Burberry's chief creative director. With his business acumen and the most glamorous of collections, Burberry Prorsum, he has taken the famous trench coat to a peak in popularity, after a period of relative stagnation. Show after show, the classic trench coat has enhanced its repertoire, introduced in neoprene or snake skin, and even a metalized version, and decorated with studs.

48 and 49 Traditionally, a trench coat is made from 26 pieces of cloth with ten buttons on its double-breasted front. Yet, somehow, it gets magically transformed and revamped every season.

British through and through and yet, surprisingly enough, very topical and cosmopolitan and a little bit cheeky like the top model who, for many seasons, was the face of the Burberry trench coat–the controversial but incomparable Kate Moss. To sum up, the trench coat was multiplied into as many variations as there are "types" and "tastes" in its present-day customers, but without losing one iota of its identity. And now, this process of diversification has developed in an extraordinary way thanks to the service offered by the Burberry Web site: customers can literally create and order their own trench coat by assembling pieces, choosing cloth, selecting details and mixing colors. To each his own (trench coat): the same as those worn by other people, yet different and unique.

50 A 1918 Burberry ad, from a time when a trench coat was basically considered to be an item of military attire.

51 By 1930 Burberry trench coats had shed their military image, as can be seen in this sophisticated and androgynous example.

A hat and trench coat: the uniform of the private detective in the entertainment world.

52 and 53 The trench coat has become "de rigueur" for private detectives in comic strips, movies and crime novels, from the well-built Dick Tracy to the bumbling Inspector Clouseau portrayed by Peter Sellers.

54 and 55 Burberry's enthusiastic adoption of electronic media is partly manifested in its "Art of the Trench" project, which features a gallery of images of devotees of the Burberry trench coat style and philosophy.

Sign in

ART OF
THE TRENCH

VIEW ALL

VIEW LATEST

SORT BY POPULARITY
☐ MOST LIKED
☐ MOST COMMENTS

GENDER
☐ WOMEN
☐ MEN

STYLING
☐ BELTED
☐ UNBELTED

TRENCH COLOUR
☐ CLASSIC SHADE
☐ DARK
☐ OTHER

WEATHER

UPLOAD YOUR TRENCH

THE ART OF THE TREN

The hat that bewitched the movies.

*A*ll types of hats have emerged from the doors of the Borsalino factory in Alessandria during the course of its more than 150 years of activity: bowlers, top hats, trilbies, fedoras, and Panamas. Hats that have covered, decorated and characterized important heads: cowboys like Clint Eastwood, blue angels like Marlene Dietrich, psychopaths like Alex DeLarge and unforgettable "tramps" like Charlie Chaplin... But there is a model of this prize-winning Italian company that has influenced the history of fashion and that, in the collective imagination, is considered to be the borsalino: the "trademark soft felt men's hat with a creased crown and average-sized brim", as it is defined in the Treccani Encyclopedia.

And even though that "b" should be a capital letter, because there is only one Borsalino and all others are mere copies of the original, the identification of this type of hat with the trademark already in 1911 was so absolute that we can overlook this tiny "error." In fact, it may even be considered a tribute.

To paraphrase one of the famous blurbs of the company–"Borsalino is synonymous with hats"–we can risk overturning the statement and say that "Hats are synonymous with Borsalino." They amount to the same thing. But behind the borsalino is "a" Borsalino: Giuseppe, who was born in Pecetto di Valenza, in the province of Alessandria, Italy, on 15 September 1834 and who laid the foundation of what was to become the empire of a company synonymous with hats throughout the world. The story of Giuseppe Borsalino is like a 19th-century Bildungsroman or "formative years" novel, but it is his true life story.

His mother, Rosa Veglio, never failed to scold him: "You have to become a hat-maker so that you'll remember you also have a head!" Aware that he had no aptitude for education, Giuseppe took this rebuke seriously and literally, as an authentic piece of advice. And, with hindsight, we can say he was right to do so. At twelve he found employment in the Camagna hat-maker's shop in Alessandria, working from the bottom up; first he was an errand boy and then an apprentice, when he moved to Sestri Ponente. He then decided to go to France, which was a leader in quality hat-

57 Jean-Paul Belmondo and Alain Delon in *Borsalino* (1970) whose title pays tribute to the legendary hat.

60 A look inside the Borsalino factory in the 1930s showing workers hand-making the famous hats.

62 and 63 The most famous bowler hat in movies, worn by Charlie Chaplin, was a Borsalino.

68 and 69 Guido Anselmi, the main character in Federico Fellini's unforgettable *8½* (1963) was partly created by the intellectual's hat worn by Marcello Mastroianni, totally different from Keith Richards' "weather-beaten" fedora.

The spirit and elegance
of Italian style is evoked
in the inimitable Fedora.

making, determined that only there would he be able to learn all the latest techniques of the craft. He went to Marseilles, Aix-en-Provence, Bordeaux and, finally, Paris, arriving there in 1850. His desire to learn, his initiative and passion, his desire to gain first-hand knowledge of the fashion world led him to seek his fortune in the French capital, where he found a job at the famous Berteil company, on Rue du Temple, which specialized in beaver-skin hats. There he learned the tricks of the trade and, in 1856, he returned to Italy with a certificate stating he was a bona fide hat-maker and could open his own workshop, which he set about doing with his newly gained experience. Waiting for him at home was his brother Lazzaro, with whom Giuseppe inaugurated their company, Borsalino Giuseppe & Fratello, on 4 April 1857 in a courtyard on Via Schiavina. From that time on the company grew at a rapid pace, thanks partly, or perhaps above all, to the iconic soft felt hat that became its hallmark. It is difficult, if not downright impossible, to establish where he got his inspiration for that particular form of hat. According to legend, the idea stemmed from the popular revolts taking place at the time. The bowlers worn by protesters ended up being dented after the violent riots, and thus lost their typical and perfect spherical shape. It seems that the characteristic "hollow" in the crown of the hat created by Giuseppe Borsalino imitated those dents, while the two side dents were designed specifically to help the cavalry take off their hats when they passed by a woman. However, perhaps the unusual shape of the borsalino was merely due to chance. In fact, it would not be surprising if that were the case.

What is certain is that the company received order after order and production rocketed. The hats, rigorously hand-made and consisting only of rabbit skin felt, which was compact but flexible, were worn by prestigious persons in the area. The ten hats produced every day proved to be insufficient

to meet demand. But at that time, like today, the production cycle for each piece, which consisted of a series of 50 consecutive phases, was about seven weeks long. Great effort and entrepreneurial courage and skill were needed in order to increase production, and Giuseppe Borsalino certainly did not lack these qualities. In 1871 he already had 130 employees and the company was making 300 hats per day. The factory was expanded, the old apparatus was replaced by more modern and efficient models, and what was a craftsman's workshop became a real factory. But what always made the difference as far as quality was concerned were the expert hands of the workers. With great acumen and far-sightedness, Borsalino understood that he should not make the domestic market his only target and that exports could become the predominant factor in the company's earnings. So he began his conquest of the world. The size of the workshop increased a great deal every time the company moved until it filled the 60,000 square meters of the historic site on the Corso Cento Cannoni that is now the home of the Borsalino Hat Museum.

When Giuseppe died the company passed to his son Terenzio and continued to grow; 1929 witnessed what could be called an epochal result, with 1.5 million hats exported out of a total of 2 million produced. The passage of time, inevitable crises, war, changes in ownership… Yet despite everything the "recent" history of Borsalino has remained the same as that inscribed in its DNA from the outset. A story of excellence and popularity that enchanted the heads of movie stars, intellectuals, politicians and icons, so much so that there was even a film, *Borsalino* (1970). It was directed by Jacques Deray and starred Alain Delon and Jean Paul Belmondo, an example of product placement so sensational that it would make even today's marketing gurus turn pale. But the story of the rise of two gangsters in Marseilles in the 1930s has very little, or nothing, to do with the mythical hat.

And the Mad Hatter?
Of course, he certainly
wore a Borsalino!

the MARiNièrE

Chanel. Simplicity becomes class.

*F*ashion also consists of stereotypes, which often also correspond to reality. For example, it is difficult to imagine an Englishman without a bowler hat and trench coat. Or an Italian woman without her tailor-made suit and a purse in her vest pocket. Or an American without jeans, sneakers and a T-shirt. These may be clichés, but they contain a basic truth. The same holds true for the cliché of the typical Frenchman or Frenchwoman, which is easy to describe: a beret, a baguette under their arms, a Gauloise cigarette in their mouth and a white shirt with blue stripes with a three-quarters sleeve and a boat neck. We need only add a bicycle to complete our picture-postcard Parisian. Certainly, the striped shirt is a deep-rooted part of the French style. It is no accident that it was the "uniform" of legendary mime Marcel Marceau; despite the constant process of subtraction and simplification that a mime adopts to create his image, the striped shirt remains a part of his "repertory."

Thanks to Mademoiselle Coco Chanel, the marinière–the French sailor's or Breton shirt–has been a constant presence in the French wardrobe for almost a century, like so many other items made in France that are timeless and continue their existence without paying heed to changing fashions. Indeed, French-made apparel is notorious for its ability to take from the universe of menswear, especially workwear, stimuli and ideas that, with slight adjustments and minor alterations, have over the years turned out to be irrepressible parts of a new type of femininity and elegance. In the early 20th-century seaside towns were overrun by an unprecedented tourist boom–both on the Atlantic coast and on the Riviera. They became extremely popular among the urban middle class, which had become acquainted with them when forced to escape bombed cities during World War I. From Saint-Tropez to Biarritz, the most fashionable seaside towns in France became haunts of aloof Parisiennes who left the hustle and bustle of their metropolis behind them. And Coco Chanel was one of them. But, unlike other women, she was not the kind of person who could simply relax and do nothing. On the contrary, she did much more than bask in the sun and launch the suntan vogue. By 1913 she had opened her first boutique outside of Paris–at Deauville,

71 Brigitte Bardot with a dazzling smile and a striped T-shirt on the set of *Viva Maria* (1965).

73 Coco Chanel at her La Pausa villa in Roquebrune-Cap-Martin, in 1930: simply chic from head to foot.

From Jean Seberg to Pablo Picasso and Jean-Paul Gaultier: part of a naval uniform becomes an icon of world culture.

in Normandy. In Paris she had already become famous thanks to her original hats. And she had acquired a clientele that followed her when, in a small boutique on the Rue Gontaut-Biron between the Gran Casinò and the luxurious Hotel Normandy, she began to propose to her faithful clients, by now habitués of this seaside resort, a carefree, comfortable, fresh item fit for dynamic, free, non-conformist women who were anything but mere "decoration" and, like her, were also very slim. This was a fashion partly inspired by the Breton shirts worn by sailors and fishermen who worked at the port, shirts that she felt were extremely chic and, paradoxically, feminine. By 1917 the striped shirt was one of the most popular Chanel products, representative of a more wide-ranging and multi-faceted "navy look" that is still highly appreciated and the object of constant revision. Decade after decade, Chanel herself wore the marinière, an irrepressible element in her casual look, which she complemented with loose-fitting slacks and low-heeled shoes. But by the time the great stylist stole the French sailor shirt from dock workers and transferred it to the wardrobes of the most up-to-date women, it had already had a long history. And, unlike so many other fashion items, it had a precise and official birthdate.

On 27 March 1858 the French Parliament passed an act that introduced the use of this singular uniform for the French Navy in Brittany. This special "uniform" was made either of knitted wool or cotton and had to be white, with 21 horizontal blue stripes (the number of Napoleon's military victories) each less than two centimeters thick. What was the reason behind this eccentric garment? It was to enable men who fell overboard to be more easily seen in the water. The transition from an item created for purely practical reasons and with a precise tone of "class", to an icon of style, was quicker and easier than one might imagine. Young French people, as well as foreigners, who had something to protest against or who simply felt the need to express their feeling of being out of place and different, wore these shirts as a sort of emblem. The marinière became the uniform of beatniks, hippies, and of the young, delicate and at the same time non-conformist actresses of the Nouvelle Vague, the cinema movement that in the early 1960s revolutionized the methods and

76-77 Pablo Picasso in 1952.

78-79 The former "wonder boy" of contemporary fashion, Jean-Paul Gaultier, in 1994. For him the Breton shirt was like a second skin, a signature, an aesthetic banner.

meanings of the seventh art. A lasting impression was made on movie audiences by the curious and tender face of the muse of the movement, Jean Seberg, who wore a marinière in Jean-Luc Godard's masterful *Breathless* (1960). But, in Francois Truffaut's "scandalous" masterpiece *Jules et Jim* (1962), another icon of French cinema, Jeanne Moreau, also wore the striped shirt, which then passed from the field of great movies to become great art. Curiously enough, Godard and Truffaut, who were perhaps those most instrumental in overturning the canons of 20th-century art, both wore the striped shirt. For Pablo Picasso the Breton shirt was a sort of second skin, a stage costume he used to construct his mythical public persona, while Andy Warhol "imposed" it on the talented people in his factory, beginning with the very fragile and glamorous Edie Sedgwick, who wore the Breton shirt–and very little else–in the hyper-experimental *Kitchen* (1965).

An artist in his own right, the most ingenious of the (former) "wonder boys" in French high fashion, Jean-Paul Gaultier, took Coco's striped shirt and radically transformed it into a trademark with his unmistakable style, often purposely provocative and shocking, for his first collection, which was presented in 1976. "Naturally, I saw the striped shirts worn by everyone: Chanel, Picasso, Brigitte Bardot," the stylist admitted, "but when I was a child my grandmother used to dress me up in one of these shirts, and so what the marinière evokes most in me is nostalgia." Nostalgia with a tinge of sensuality, we must add. Because a part of the world of stripes created by Gaultier is the extremely popular perfume Le Male, launched in 1994, whose packaging is a powerful male torso on which is a stylized Breton shirt, which is an allusion to tempting, "sinful" nudity. What partly inspired the great stylist was the homoerotic desire as narrated by the most cultivated film directors. From Luchino Visconti's highly refined attraction *Death in Venice* (1971)–in which the object of Gustav von Aschenbach's tragic and painful desire, the beautiful, ephebic Tadzio, wears a Breton shirt–to the more titillating and twilight desire in *Querelle* (1982), Rainer Werner Fassbinder's last film, in which Brad Davis projects in the collective erotic imagination the figure of the macho and gay sailor who always wears a marinière. It is as if we have somehow come full circle.

CHANEL N5

More than a perfume, a milestone of seduction.

> *"I always launch my collection on the fifth day of the fifth month of the year, so this number brings me luck."*
> *Coco Chanel*

Risking sacrilege, one could say that there was a pre-N°5 epoch and a post-N°5 epoch. Evidently not satisfied with having revolutionized the history of fashion in a radical and irreversible manner with her couture clothing creations, which were manifestos of freedom, comfort and dynamism, Coco Chanel overturned the perfume industry as well. She needed only one perfume to make sure that nothing would remain as it had been, and that what had until then been in vogue would suddenly seem to be outdated. Her mission was to undermine conventions and her credo was to violate rules. A philosophy and an aesthetic that even a simple fragrance could embody.

Monte Carlo, summer 1921. The already famous stylist is in company with her pianist friend Misia Sert, one of the leading members of the most popular circle of Parisian artists, her painter husband José Maria Sert, and the Grand Duke Dmitri Pavlovich of Russia, the czar's cousin. Like almost all ingenious ideas, that of creating a perfume was triggered by a normal conversation. Not that the idea of a celebrated fashion designer setting about creating a perfume was wholly original. Paul Poiret had attempted to do so ten years earlier, but with rather disappointing results. And, in fact, Coco was reluctant to take a plunge in a sector with which she was unfamiliar. But if there was one thing Chanel liked, it was a challenge, especially a difficult one. Thus, Coco's approach to this adventure was totally and predictably original. "I want to offer women an artificial perfume," she declared. "Yes, I really do mean artificial, like a dress, something that has been made. I don't want any rose or lily of the valley, I want a perfume that is a composition."

The break with tradition was violent. The first perfume that Maison Chanel produced was not to be similar in any way to other perfumes then in vogue: concentrated, intense, at times nauseating, made of immediately recognizable natural floral fragrances. Romantic, monotonous, unvarying perfumes were not for Coco. She wanted to invent, not reproduce. She wanted to originate a vision, not a duplicate. And she wanted to surprise, not reassure. The person who made the couturier's intuition a reality was the perfumier Ernest Beaux, who was introduced to Coco by Grand Duke Dmitri. Born in Moscow in 1881 to French parents, at seventeen Beaux began to work for A. Rallet & Co., the leading French perfumery in Russia, which boasted the czar's court among its most prestigious clients.

81 Marilyn Monroe in 1955 with a bottle of perfume for which she inadvertently did testimonial advertising by stating that the only thing she wore to bed was five drops of Chanel N°5.

83 A 1923 caricature of Coco Chanel, and her iconic bottle of perfume, drawn by Georges Goursat.

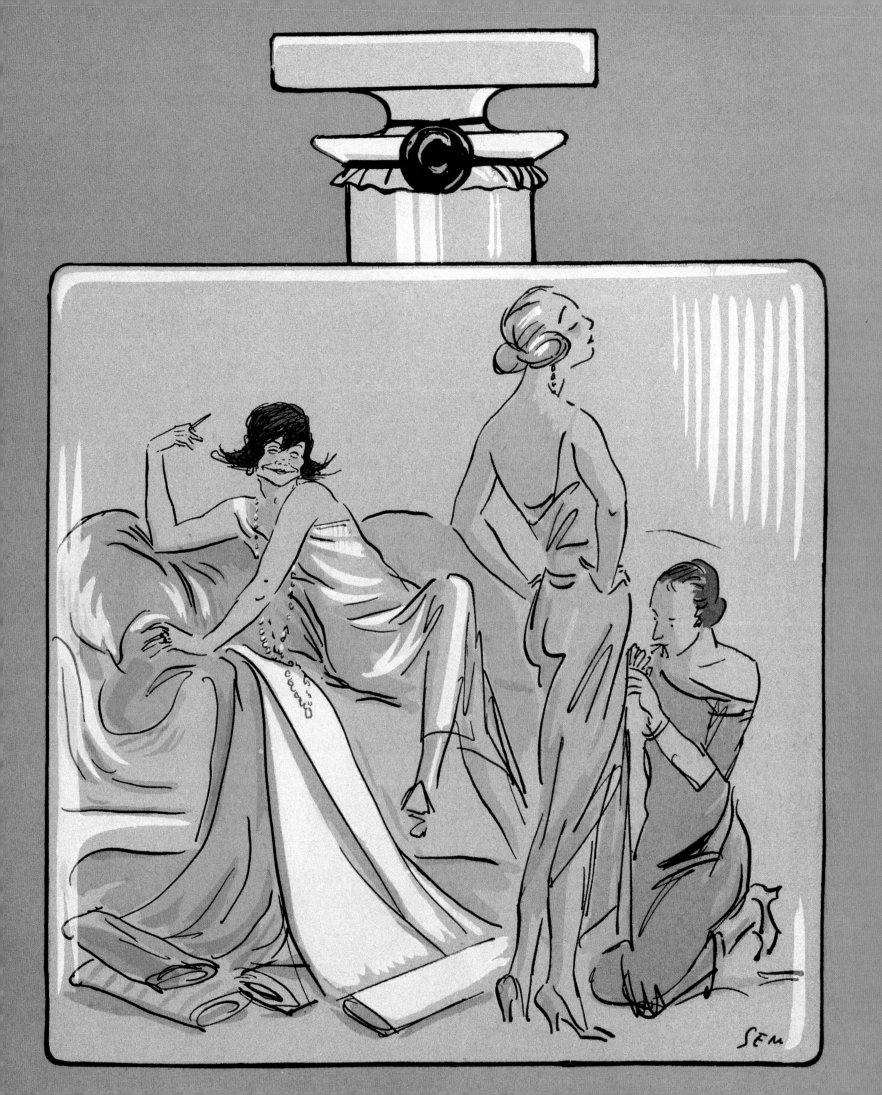

Coco met him at La Bocca, near Grasse, historic center of the French perfume industry, where he had set up his laboratory, studied, and elaborated and created his innovative perfumes. Coco made very precise requests: she wanted a perfume that was nothing at all like those already on the market, a perfume that was to be both elegant and luxurious, opulent but simple, delicate but persistent, feminine but not saccharine; a perfume that smelled good and was reminiscent of women. Beaux could not wait to put into practice his revolutionary research on aldehydes, organic compounds of synthetic origin that were extremely volatile and were able to make floral scents persistent but light at the same time. Up to that time the perfume industry had exploited the potential of aldehydes much too timidly, while Beaux's work was based on them. Aldehydes were the linchpin of the Copernican revolution of perfume that Mademoiselle Chanel had begun to plan. Inspiration came to Beaux's talented nose from the memory of a trip he had made during World War I: the scent of the lakes and rivers of the northern countries in the midday sun. Like a slightly mad scientist, he began mixing various components to a much greater degree and number than was usual at the time. At the end of his experiments he presented Coco Chanel with two series of samples that were identified only by numbers, from one to five and from twenty to twenty-four. What struck Coco was an articulated symphony of heterogeneous notes, none of which really prevailed over the others. A rich floral scent consisting of no less than 80 elements and made even more intense by the massive use of aldehydes. One could smell the exotic ylang-ylang, the delicate pink May rose, the sublime neroli of Grasse. And then, almost by surprise, there arrived the scents of sandalwood, vanilla and vetiver. The fragrances were in a harmonious blend that included them all but in which no single one predominated. A concentration of sensuality, a distillation of the eternally feminine that words cannot describe. The objective had been achieved. Coco asked for more jasmine, the noblest and most luxurious of essences, but her choice was sure: the first Chanel perfume would be N°5.

Indeed, this perfume was so unusual that it could not but have an equally unusual name. She rejected melodramatic suggestions and passionate allusions to the perfumes then in vogue. Chanel did not want a new French "Le Sang Francais" or "Le Fruit Defendu"; she did not want a name that was languid, insupportable, obtrusive romantic slush. Her choice was the most essential name: N°5. After all, wasn't that the "name" of the sample Beaux had proposed? She relied on chance; moreover, five had always been her lucky number. Even the bottle in which she chose to launch the new fragrance was more like an aseptic, square laboratory test tube than one of the sculptured and hyper-decorated creations, in the style of Lalique, used so much by other perfumiers: a parallelepiped on which appeared the most sober and austere logo, a rigid black and white rectangle that, except for some very minor changes, has remained unchanged to the present day. The bottle was so modern that it earned a place in the Museum of Modern Art in New York and bewitched the father of modernity himself, Andy Warhol, who immortalized it in a series of silk-screens, on an equal level with his beloved icons, popular 20th-century stars.

N°5 enjoyed immediate and worldwide success, due partly to the sophisticated marketing strategy that Mademoiselle Chanel adopted, well ahead of her time, with such extraordinary intuition and far-sightedness.

At first, N°5 was not sold but was given away, almost like a prize, to the Maison's most faithful clients and to Coco's intimate friends. So it was that the perfume immediately became a must-have among Parisian high socie-

ty, something plush that a certain class of woman simply could not do without. Despite its rather high price already in the 1920s, it sold more bottles than all the other fragrances, almost one bottle per minute, a record it has maintained to this day. Perhaps in order to encourage such exceptional consumption, Coco herself invited women to "overindulge." "People tell me that I smell nice: I wear perfume!" the stylist admitted, harshly criticizing her fellow countrymen. "The French put a drop behind each ear. A small bottle lasts six months. And they call it being perfumed!" Success did not decline even during the immediate postwar period, when, despite the fact that Maison Chanel had closed down, N°5 continued to be sold in amazingly large quantities, even to American soldiers who wanted to buy at least one bottle to take back home to their girlfriends.

And was it precisely in the United States that N°5 would find its most famous and perfect fan, the quintessence of femininity, so fragile and yet disturbing; only Marilyn Monroe could epitomize the fascination of this terribly complex fragrance. When, in 1954, a journalist asked Monroe what she wore when she went to bed, she replied, with a tone halfway between the ironic and the serious: "Only five drops of Chanel." This

was enough to spark the most allusive thoughts and to transform the perfume into a myth. But there were many actresses who became spokeswomen for Chanel N°5 publicity campaigns. Candice Bergen, Ali Mac-Graw, Lauren Hutton, Catherine Deneuve, Carole Bouquet, Nicole Kidman and Audrey Tatou: stars with a sophisticated beauty that is never banal, women with evident caliber and a strong, nonconformist personality, the only ones who could embody the spirit of such an important and demanding perfume.

After a series of such special women, only a man could have been considered equal to the task. And what a man: today N°5 is identified with Brad Pitt, in the latest portrayal of a totally original publicity campaign. As the commercial suggests, this is an inevitable combination, because nowadays perhaps only a man can testify to the power of the most feminine of a woman's instruments of seduction.

86 and 87 American soldiers in 1945 standing in line in front of the Chanel boutique in Paris. Their girlfriends back home were expecting a bottle of N°5, as were the members of the American Women's Auxiliary Army Corps who bought this perfume in liberated Paris in August 1944.

88-89 Like a star, Chanel N°5 was portrayed by the genius of Pop Art, Andy Warhol, in 1985.

Catherine Deneuve for Chanel

From the NBA to streetwear.

*T*his brand name is familiar to many, if not to everyone–those who, at least once in their lifetime, have heard of Charles "Chuck" Hollis Taylor. We are ready to bet that not many would be able to say much about his life but that they would at least know that he had something to do with sports, especially basketball. Chuck Taylor was not only a basketball player. He was certainly not a basketball champion, yet he was closely connected to this extremely popular American sport. Taylor was born in Azalia, Indiana in 1901. He wasn't particularly tall and not particularly slim. But despite this, from the time he was an adolescent he was passionate about basketball. He practiced incessantly and by the time he attended Columbus High School in Indiana he had attracted attention as a potentially good player. A distinguishing feature of his playing "style" was that he always wore brown Converse All Star shoes, with thick rubber soles and high canvas uppers, because he was convinced that their superior quality enhanced his performance on court.

The company that manufactured these sneakers was the Converse Rubber Corporation of Malden, Massachusetts, founded in 1908 by Marquis Mills Converse, and initially specializing in rubber galoshes, boots, and shoes. According to popular legend, the idea of producing this type of item came to him after he tumbled down a wet stairway. His mission was to create shoes that would guarantee Maximum Traction, the company's motto; the feet had to be solidly and safely planted on the floor. Converse shoes were also popular with fishermen as well as aficionados of camping, and they became a free-time must-have. However, the 4,000 shoes that the company manufactured every day were not enough, and Converse felt it had to expand and diversify its business to other sectors. Consequently, in 1917, it produced the first sports shoes conceived specifically for basketball players, which were called All Star sneakers. This relatively young sport was already very popular in the United States and almost all youngsters shooting the ball into the hoop every afternoon. One of them was Chuck Taylor.

Calling him a fan of these shoes does not do justice to his passion and dedication. In 1921, Taylor went to the Converse sales offices in Chicago in search of a job. His faith in sneakers must have been enough to convince the director, S.R. "Bob" Peltz, to hire him immediately as a salesman. From that moment on Chuck Taylor and Converse All Star were one and the same. It does not matter so much that

95 A young Edmund Hillary wearing worn-out All Star sneakers while having his photograph taken among the inhabitants of a Himalayan village.

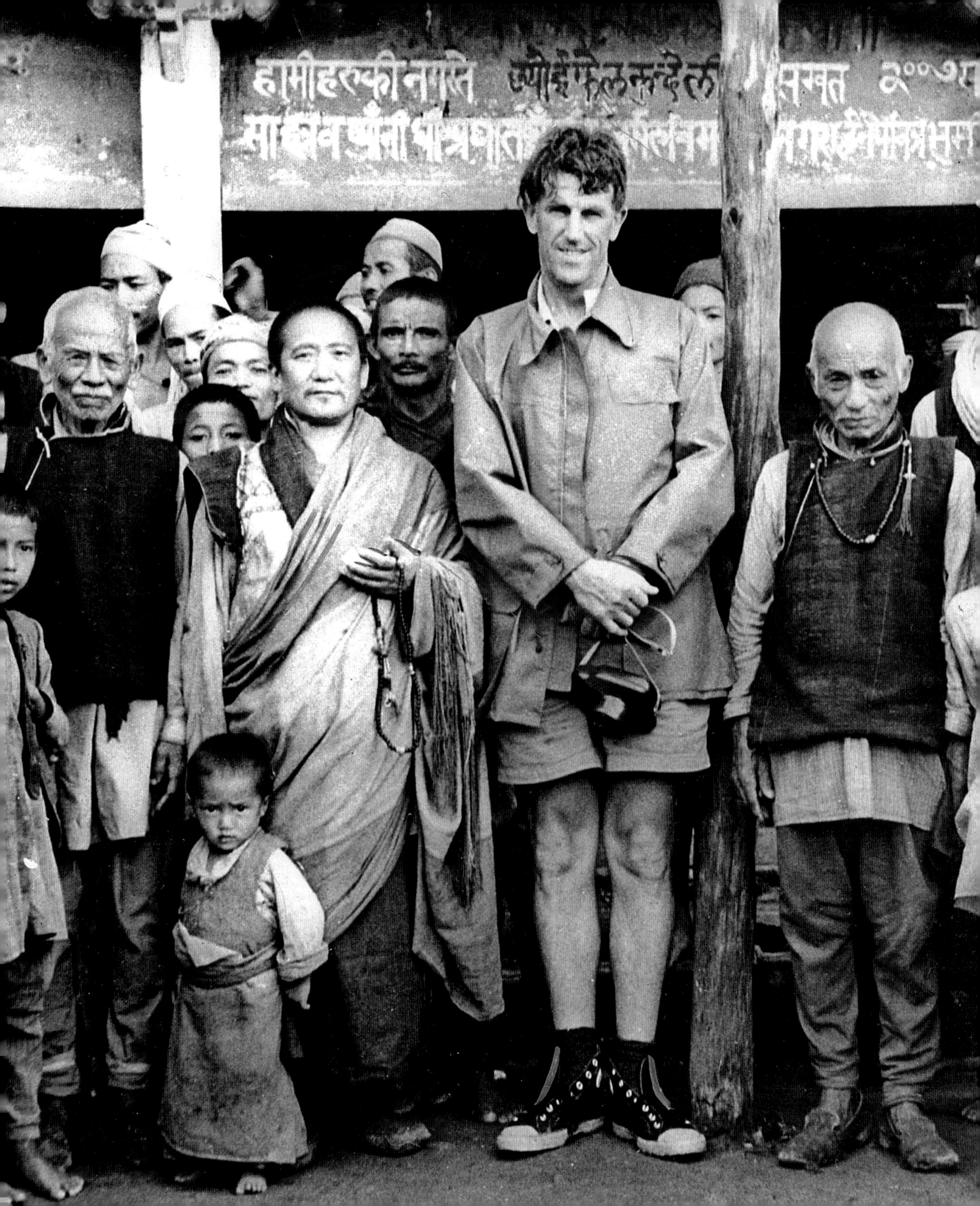

Taylor was not the star of major professional basketball teams that his anonymous biography claimed. His contribution to the sport was even more far-reaching. In fact, in 1923, thanks to his advice and suggestions the company made some improvements to its most famous product that increased its flexibility, support, and comfort, transforming it first into an icon of basketball courts and then into the myth of daily life that we still love throughout the world. Since the shoe was considered to be the result of Taylor's intelligence and experience, in 1932 the young man had the honor of seeing his signature put on the shoe, which from then on was known as the "Chuck Taylor All Star." To this day his signature can be seen on the sneaker logo, near the familiar star.

But Chuck Taylor's contribution to this beloved sport went even further. For almost fifty years, until his death in 1969, he was the greatest advocate and promoter of basketball in the United States. Mr. Basketball, as he was called, went everywhere, in his white Cadillac, from state to state, from city to city, and from one university campus to another. His mission was to make people aware of basketball and to look for talented young players whom he would then recommend to coaches of leading university teams; he also organized basketball clinics. Interest in the sport increased and players became "pets" of the public. Another ingenious idea of Taylor's, lying somewhere between marketing and mythology, helped publicize the world of basketball stars: the Converse Basketball Yearbook, first published in 1922. It featured photographs of the most famous players and coaches in the country, all of whom naturally wore the popular All Star sneakers. Indeed, in time, basketball and Chuck Taylor sneakers were virtually synonymous, and the popularity and promotion of both increased exponentially. And again it was Taylor who, in 1936, designed patriotic sneakers–white (for the first time) with red and blue details–for American athletes participating in the 1936 Berlin Olympic Games. The All Star monopoly spread to other fields. World War II did not stop the company's success as it began to produce shoes that could be used by US troops at the front. If sneakers were popular in the 1950s they were even more popular in the 1960s; whether on basketball courts or on the streets, people loved them. Wilt Chamberlain, the great Philadelphia Warriors star, wore All Star sneakers on 2 March 1962, when he scored a record 100 points in a single game,

More than a champion, more than a fan, Chuck Taylor was a true ambassador for the All Star trademark.

an achievement unequalled for many years. But another record belonged to Converse. At the beginning of the decade it controlled a huge share of the market, an incredible 90%.

Although they may seem almost rudimentary to us today, especially if compared with the aerodynamic, high-tech sneakers produced nowadays, for many years Converse shoes were the most technically sophisticated that professional players could ask for.

The Converse domination on basketball courts began to falter when aggressive competitors launched and won the innovation battle and won. But this decline on the basketball court was countered by a triumph among the public at large off the court. The official NBA shoes became a cult object for an entire generation and has remained so to this day. In fact, even a counter-culture actress like Kristen Stewart, who played Bella Swan in the Twilight series, wore them on the red carpet of the premiere of the fifth episode of the saga together with a very *bon ton* red sheath dress designed by Yigal Azrouël. Young people like her (and not only young people) are passionate about the Chucks, perhaps because they have managed to retain their obstinately vintage appeal. All Star sneakers enjoyed a second childhood in the 1980s thanks to rock and punk music, and above all in the 1990s, when they, along with Dr. Martens boots, became the iconic footware of Generation X: down-at-heel and worn-out, exactly as youngsters from Seattle to Europe preferred. They were a favorite of Kurt Cobain, the "father" of grunge. Fashions change, and very quickly, especially in recent years, but All Star sneakers are always the same, as are their fans, because admittedly that getting rid of your Chuck Taylors is always a traumatic experience; even when they are nearly falling to pieces with every step you take, they always seem to be beautiful and irreplaceable. The immaculate, new Chucks on display in shop windows are not as fascinating as the ones that have been weathered by walking, at concerts, in escapades–this is something that occurs with no other fashion accessory. The rubber needs to be dirty; the canvas–nowadays highly colored–must adapt to one's foot and absorb its shape; the laces must lose their brilliant white hue. In other words, these shoes must be lived in.

98 and 99 All Stars became punk when worn by Dee Dee Ramone, bassist of the Ramones, and a symbol of non-conformity when Mick Jagger wore a pair of Converse sneakers to marry Bianca.

100-101 Andy Warhol's *Converse extra special value* (1986) attests to the fact that All Star sneakers became an integral part of pop culture.

A "crocodile" that became a trademark.

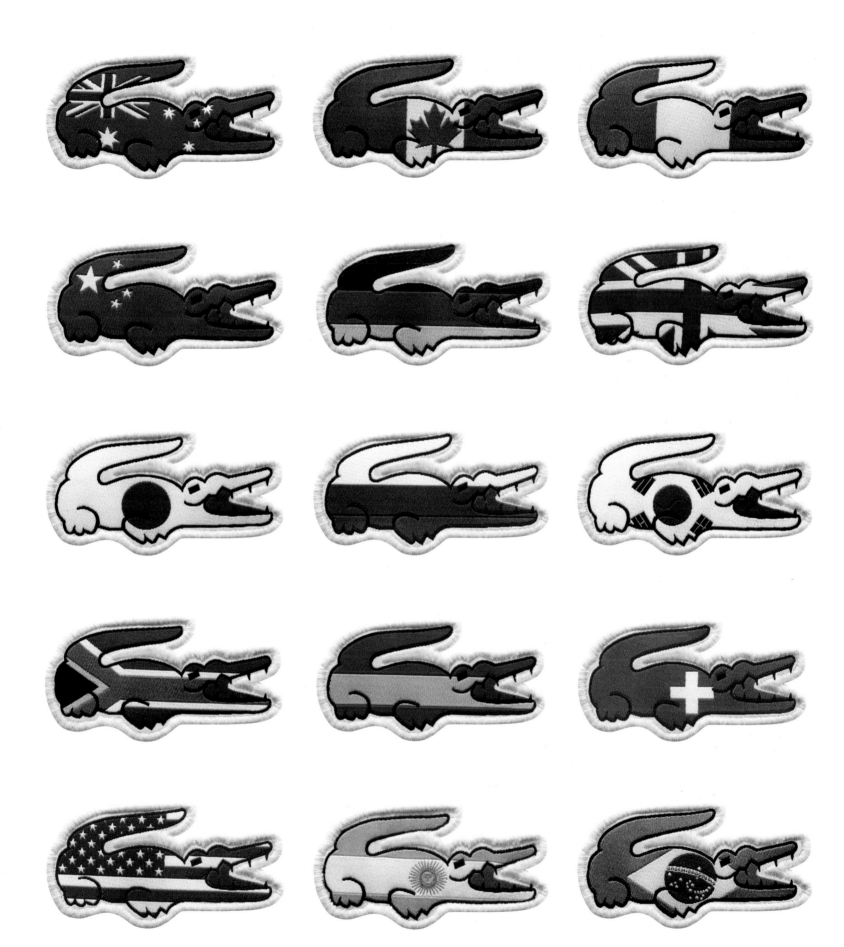

*T*here are certain people who are destined for success, people who are able to reinvent their life, plunge into new adventures, and succeed in whatever enterprise they tackle. These people are never content; furthermore, they are born achievers.

René Lacoste was one of these people. His life story was marked by determination, unwavering purpose and, it must be said, luck. He was born in Paris in 1904, at a time when tennis was extremely popular. The modern codification of the game had only recently been formalized. Tennis was an elegant, patrician, and refined sport, both in its gestures and aesthetic, a direct descendant of "royal tennis", which had been the passion of 13th-century Italian noblemen and was a sport different from all others. In the early 1900s, tennis attracted and entertained people around the world. In the space of just a few years, between 1877 and 1908, the most important tennis tournaments, the so-called Grand Slam tournaments, had been established: Wimbledon, the US Open, the French Open and the Australian Open. In 1900, the United States and Great Britain played against each other in the first Davis Cup. In 1913, twelve national tennis federations merged, giving rise to the first International Tennis Federation.

Lacoste believed in sport. His father Jean-Jules, a manager at the Hispano-Suiza auto company, was a finalist in the first French national canoeing championship, held in 1890, so he could not have objected too much when his son René fell in love with tennis during a trip to Britain. The boy was already fifteen at the time and had no innate vocation for the sport. Despite the fact that tennis, at that time, was purely for amateurs, Jean-Jules supported and encouraged his son; money was no object in the Lacoste family.

His confidence was rewarded with results. In 1921, when he was only seventeen, René won his first important junior tournament. His playing style was clear from the outset. Lacoste was a player with a great analytical gift. He studied his opponent, tried to upset his game, and was able to pick out and recognize any variables and any constants. With all this in mind he moved around the court in such a way as to be able to foresee his opponent's moves and "tricks" – in other words, his opponent's style. Lacoste was a strategist. Yet, although his tactics and strategy were brilliant, his technique was no less so. His best shots were

103 From the iconic green to the bright colors of the flags of half the world: this is the Lacoste tribute to the 2012 Olympic Games.

105 The famous crocodile logo of the company founded by tennis player René Lacoste, seen in this 1930s ad (left),
is a reference to his on-court nickname.

1 9 3 3

POUR
LE TENNIS
LE GOLF
LA PLAGE

LES VÉRITABLES

"CHEMISES LACOSTE"

PORTENT LA MARQUE

CHEMISE LACOSTE

R. LACOSTE ET A. GILLIER

from the baseline, especially his almost perfect backhand. Journalists commented on his first victory by stating that he had everything it took to become an excellent tennis player and that he would be a world class champion. They were, perhaps, unaware of how prophetic their words were.

Natural tennis talent may not have been in his DNA, but his determination and commitment demonstrated how one can succeed despite this. And he responded to his instructors and coaches' reproaches by working on inventing a tennis ball machine, which he patented in 1927. If you want something done, do it yourself. Lacoste's career started off on the right foot, with victory after victory. In 1922 he played in the world clay-court championship, and the following year he participated in his first Davis Cup, during which, as he himself recalled, he was given the nickname that would become his "brand name": the crocodile. He was walking through the streets of Boston with French team captain, Pierre Gillou. They stopped in front of a leather goods store window, and Gillou said he would give him a precious alligator skin suitcase if he won that afternoon's match. Lacoste lost it, in fact, but a journalist heard about the anecdote: what better nickname could there be for a player than that of a tenacious reptile that never lets go?

With an extraordinary marketing idea that was at once naïve and very shrewd, Lacoste asked his stylist friend, Robert George, to sew a crocodile, with gaping jaws, onto the lapel of a sports blazer. This was logical, because like his colleagues, Lacoste went onto the clay courts dressed in a kind of uniform that had to

106 and 107 René Lacoste in action at the height of his career. Clearly visible on his jacket lapel is the reptile that would become famous as the logo of his company.

be white. Accustomed as we are to plastic material, fluorescent colors and aerodynamic shapes and lines, the "respectable" attire of that time make us smile and seems almost prehistoric: flannel trousers and belt, long-sleeved shirt, tie, V-necked pullover, jacket, and hat with a cloth visor. Attire that is perhaps not ideal for sport, but decidedly stylish, especially when worn by René, with its crocodile emblem, which made all the difference.

Lacoste gradually reached the top of the international rankings. In 1924 he was the leading player in France. The following year he was blessed by the gods, and won the French Open and the Wimbledon singles titles. His list of prestigious victories and prizes became longer and longer. Together with Jacques Brugnon, Henri Cochet and Jean Borotra he formed the matchless David Cup team known as the Four Musketeers, which from 1927 to 1932 won virtually everything there was to win.

While his playing style on court won unanimous acclaim, his new tennis attire provoked a scandal. In order to combat the heat on American courts, in 1926 he had begun to wear a strange combination of T-shirt and shirt, a piqué cotton shirt (with a jersey petit piqué weave) that was called polo because of its similarity to shirts worn in that equestrian sport. The new shirt had the short sleeves of the T-shirt, which until then had been worn only as underwear, and the collar and buttoning of a normal shirt. In this case, one plus one makes three. The shirt tail was slightly longer so that it would stay tucked in. The polo was a combination of technology, comfort, and elegance. However, the French Tennis Federation considered it to be indecent. But Lacoste continued to wear it.

René's career had its ups and downs and then ended abruptly. In 1929 he won the French Open, after which, officially, chronic bronchitis put an end to his playing career. In

subsequent years, he returned to the tennis court and, subsequently, became the French Davis Cup team coach and the president of the French Tennis Federation. But he knew that his future lay elsewhere. Today, it seems quite natural for a sports champion to become a brand name and to exploit his image commercially. But for Lacoste, in 1933, it was both pioneering and ingenious. The former champion believed that the polo shirt could be worn by anybody, athletes and non-athletes alike. With his friend André Gillier, owner and president of the largest French knitwear manufacturing company at the time, he founded the Chemise Lacoste sportswear company. The featured item in their catalog was the L.12.12, the inimitable tennis shirt identified with the former tennis champion Lacoste. The crocodile, no longer a mere nickname, had become a logo. And it seems that this was the first time a logo had been visible and actually exhibited on clothing.

The explosion of casual wear in the 1960s used the Lacoste polo shirt as the tool to disrupt the old coordinates and old-fashioned canons of elegance. Starting on the tennis court, the shirt has become a staple in wardrobes throughout the world. Once only white, it now offers a virtually infinite range of colors. And once a "technical, specialist" item, it is now worn on almost all occasions and at all times. Even under a double-breasted jacket.

From the court and the field, the polo shirt became part of the world's wardrobe as a symbol of elegance.

This was the first time a logo was so noticeable, or rather, exhibited, on clothing.

110 A scarf, large sunglasses and white Lacoste shirt. Simplicity suffused with class, according to Jackie Kennedy, seen here in 1968.

111 Clint Eastwood discards the cowboy attire he wears in movies and dons casual Lacoste apparel.

ADRIEN BRODY

UNCONVENTIONAL CHIC

LACOSTE

112-113 Formerly an item of sportswear, the polo shirt may
now be worn casually at any time and on any occasion, even
under a jacket, as actor Adrien Brody elegantly demonstrates in
this recent Lacoste ad.

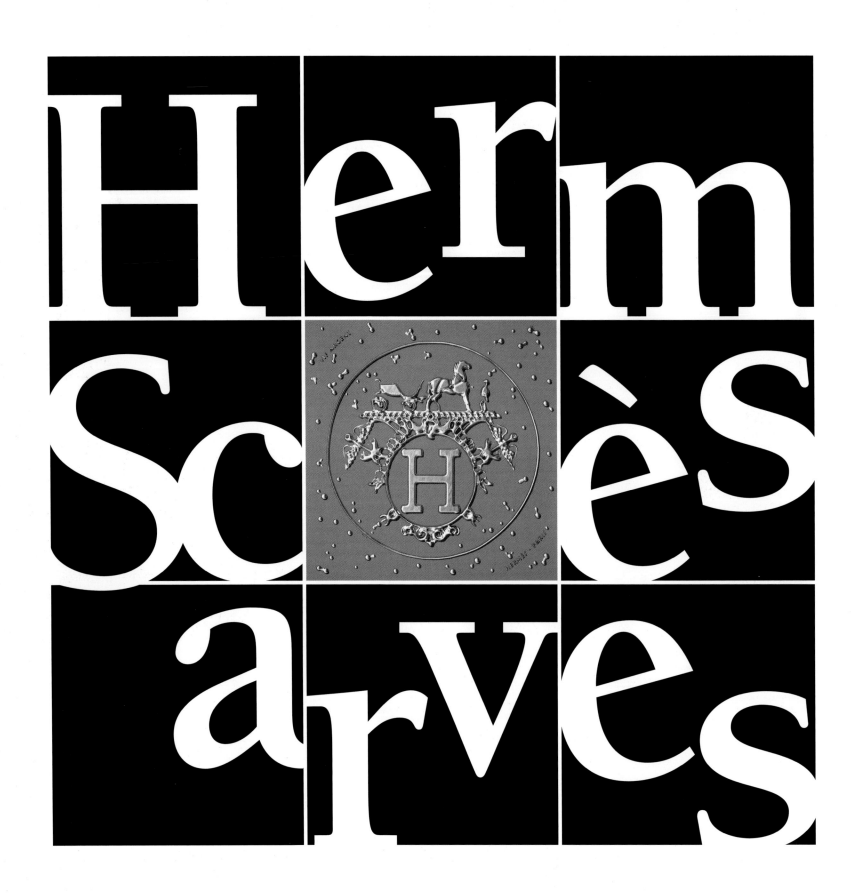

Hermès Scarves

A silk rainbow.

BRIDES de GALA
par
HERMÈS
PARIS

Carré: a name derived from its square shape and which became synonymous with elegance, transcending passing fashions, seasons and trends.

In 1959 Grace Kelly, a princess of style and a de facto princess, wore one when she took a Mediterranean cruise aboard Aristotle Onassis's yacht, using it as a sling for her right arm, which had suffered an infection. The paparazzi immortalized her, always elegant and smiling, in her immaculate dress, as befits a star who is capable of transforming an ailment into a pretext for displaying her glamor. On the other side of the English Channel, at about the same time, Her Majesty Queen Elizabeth II, wore one while posing for a portrait, which would later be immortalized on a postage stamp. A few decades later, during her long walks with her corgis, she wore a Hermès scarf as a headscarf – either out of habit or for effect, as Audrey Hepburn did, or out of necessity, considering the proverbially damp and windy British climate.

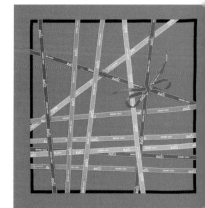

A few decades later, Sharon Stone–or better, Catherine Trammel–used a white one in a totally different–and unimaginable–way in *Basic Instinct* (1992): to immobilize former rock star Johnny Boz, in a morbid sex game before brutally killing him with an ice pick. And white is also the color of the one that the equally but differently treacherous Miranda Priestley, the modern anti-heroine of *The Devil Wears Prada* (2006), cannot do without–a fetish similar to that of Linus and his blanket. If the manager (Meryl Streep) of the imaginary Bible of fashion, Runway, is "addicted" to it, then the Hermès scarf is really an irrepressible totem of elegance of the past and the present.

This product of the legendary Parisian Maison Hermès is not a mere scarf. It is a Carré, so radically different, even in name, from other accessories that might seem to have a similar function. While the word "foulard" smacks a little of "old maid", Carré immediately calls to mind an irresistibly aloof lady of understated elegance above and beyond the trends of the moment and the seasons. The noun Carré is derived from its rigorously square shape, which it has had since 1937, when the brothers-in-law Robert Dumas and Jean René Guerrand, members by marriage of the fourth generation of the great Hermès family, put the first Carré on sale. Exactly 100 years had passed since the time when Thierry Hermès–a Protestant of humble origins, born in Krefeld, Germany in 1801 and who moved to Paris in the 1820s–founded a saddlery company that, in time, became one of the world's leading manufacturers of quality leather goods. It then began producing fashion and luxury goods, of which it is still one of the few bastions, despite the present world economic crisis.

116 and 117 Standing out among some of the most famous Hermès motifs is *Brides de Gala* (1957) (left), the most popular of all.

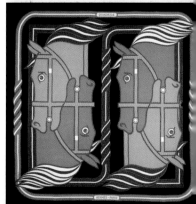

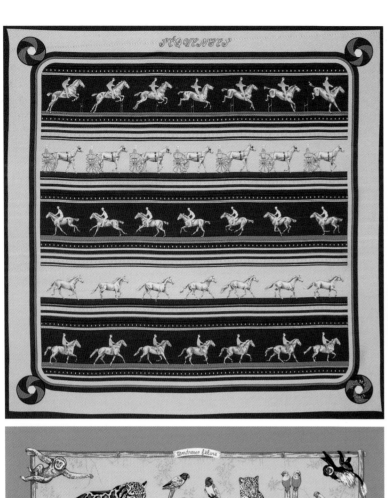

118 Other Hermès motifs from among hundreds they have created, including *Des omnibus et Dames Blanches* (1937), (above right), the "founding father" of a very long series.

The Carré details: 35 x 35 inches, 2.4 miles of silk thread and weighing only 2.29 ounces.

This is not to say that the two brothers-in-law consciously planned to celebrate this anniversary in a grandiose and memorable way. And it seems almost certain that they did not aim at creating an icon of modern bourgeois elegance. Nothing in the history of Hermès was the result of theory or mere strategy. The greatest, most triumphal successes of this company stemmed from simple, almost banal intuition, and perhaps even more from pure chance. This was the case with the Carré: the idea was to utilize the same silk already employed to produce jockeys' shirts–which drew inspiration from handkerchiefs used by Napoleon's soldiers–but now targeted at the multifarious vanity of a female clientele.

Yet, as it was always nonconformist, Hermès did not utilize the geometric patterns so much in vogue at that time for their first Carré, which, like all the future ones, had a name: *Jeu des Omnibus et Dames Blanches*. In the area enclosed by two concentric circles is a series of twelve horse-drawn buses of the Entreprise des Omnibus, ancestor of the modern public transport system, moving at a speed that at the time must have seemed sheer folly. In the innermost circle, seated around a table, is a group of men and women enjoying a popular parlor game based precisely on the heated competition that arose in the 1830s among city transport companies–which were founded, by coincidence, just when Thierry, in Paris, was beginning to cultivate the idea of establishing his small company.

The real success of the Carré arrived only some years later when, in 1948, the destiny of the iconic accessory crossed paths with that of Marcel Gandit, the inventor of the inimitable Lyonnaise method of silk square printing, a unique and unequalled technique in terms of precision, definition and brilliance of color, thanks to the high degree of craftsmanship, which the Maison still persists in using. It is the expert hands of craftsmen that dye, one nuance of pigment at a time, the long skein of silk that yields 100 Carrés at a time. By means of a series of successive screens–as many as there are colors in each of the illustrations (there may be more than 40)–the areas of the different colors interlock, as in an intangible mosaic.

The outcome of such patient and meticulous work is the silk scarf measuring 90 x 90 centimeters (35 x 35 inches) and weighing only 65 grams (2.2 ounces), the equivalent of four kilometers of silk thread produced by 250 silkworms. Its *de rigueur* finish consists of the unmistakable hand-rolled and hand-stitched hems of the roulottage. A square of precious fabric that is something like a mirror or canvas. Like a mirror because–having remained faithful to itself despite the passage of so many decades–it reflects the more than 100 years of Hermès history. Its symbols, its allegories, its favorite motifs and its manias, all re-surface periodically, continuously re-invented. These include harnesses and horses, arms

and hunting scenes, carriages and boats, flowers and feathers, soldiers in full dress uniforms, exotic cultures such as those of Native and African Americans, the sky and the sea. To sum up, the cosmos, which pulsates inside and outside the world of Hermès.

In its aristocratic refinement, the Carré is even a paradoxically democratic and "transgenerational" accessory because for two generations (at least) it has delighted mothers as much as daughters. While the former wrap them around their throats with simulated nonchalance à la Grace Kelly, the latter use them to create anachronistic hippie turbans, slightly decorative belts or improvised deluxe tops. They are both equally respectful of the advice on the Hermès scarf uttered by that genius of fashion Diana Vreeland, the legendary fashion editor: "Wear it in the morning, knotting it around your throat before going out. It imparts so much elegance that there's no need to look at oneself in the mirror." In short, there is so much supply because of so much demand. They say that one Carré is sold every twenty seconds throughout the world.

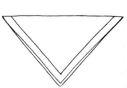

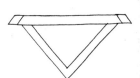

120 and 121 Brigitte Bardot and Her Majesty Queen Elizabeth II: two totally different women who consider the Hermès scarf to be an indispensable accessory.

GÉOMÉTRIE CRÉTOISE

HERMÈS-PARIS

123 top One phase in the complex and labor-intensive process of printing a Hermès scarf.

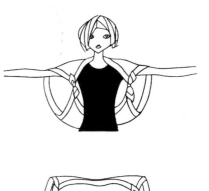

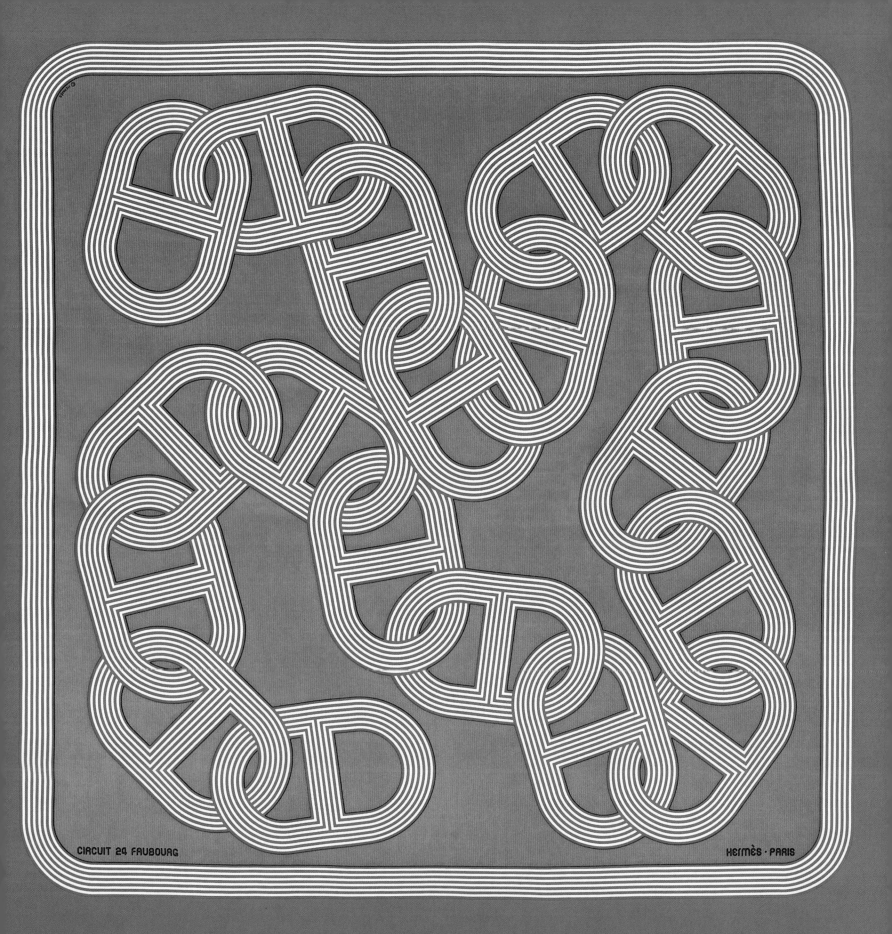

CIRCUIT 24 FAUBOURG HERMÈS · PARIS

BALLeRiNas

Dance classes on city streets.

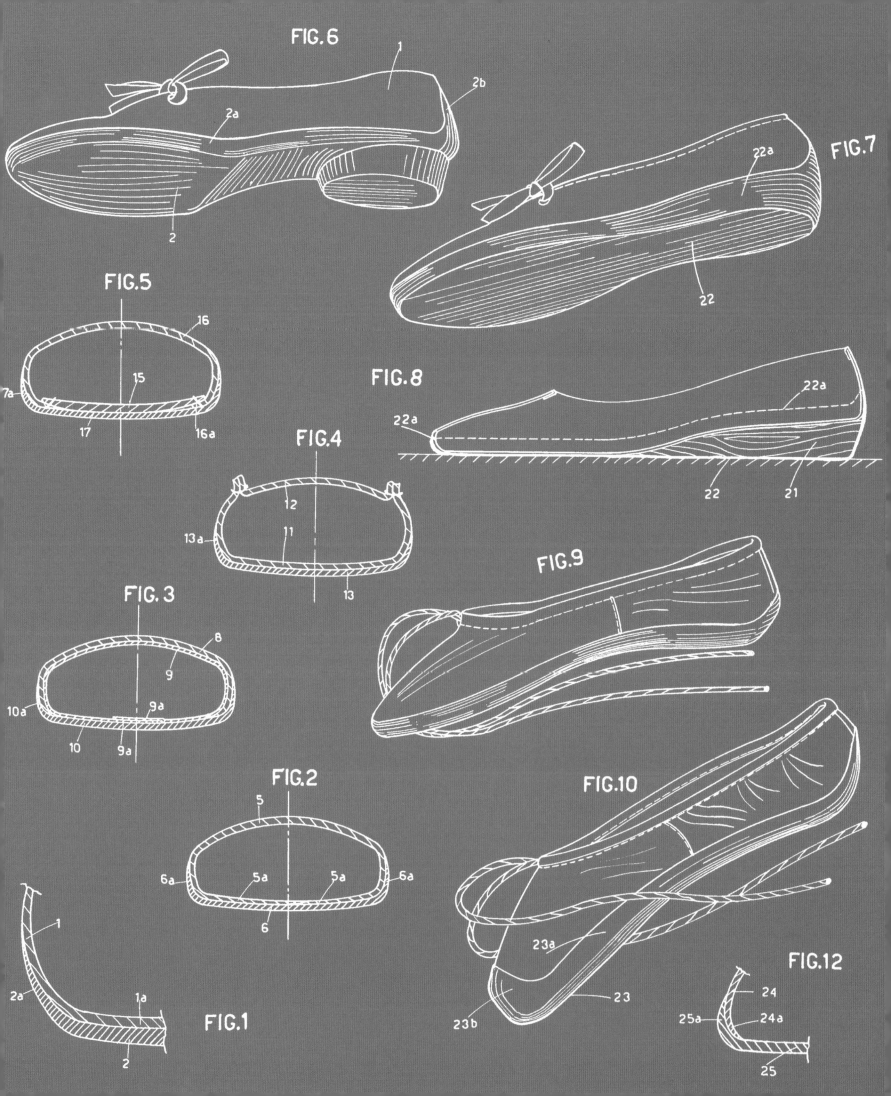

FIG.6

FIG.7

FIG.5

FIG.8

FIG.4

FIG.3

FIG.9

FIG.2

FIG.10

FIG.12

FIG.1

*T*hese popular shoes are the living and undisputable proof that women are not deceived that easily and that not even fashion, the great illusion par excellence, can dupe them.

According to the reliable and influential British daily newspaper, *The Guardian*, in the first quarter of 2012 world-famous department store Marks & Spencer sold something like 100,000 ballerina flats, 76% more than the preceding year, despite the economic crisis. And they could have sold even more. The same thing was true with the equally popular John Lewis chain: in August 2012 more than twice as many ballerinas were sold than in the same month of the preceding year. They are not exactly "disposables", but the way they are bought does indicate, in a certain sense, that type of purchase. One buys ballerinas because they are useful, like underwear. They are almost a kind of necessity.

But this phenomenon is by no means limited to the mass market. Quite the contrary. On the pages of magazines, whether glossy or not, ballerinas are the rage among today's stars, who wear them during their leisure time, when they take their children to school or pick them up, or when they go to buy milk at the supermarket. They wear them while taking a stroll in the park or filling up the gas tank of their flashy car, or even when they pop out for a few minutes, have themselves photographed, and end up on the pages of magazines. Their outfit is rather limited, with little margin for creativity: slim fit jeans, an artfully torn T-shirt, and a designer jacket. And, naturally, the inevitable handbag–designer label, recognizable and expensive. The pioneers of this trend, back when things were quite different, were Kate Moss and Sienna Miller, that is to say, the high priestesses of shabby chic, the only style, objectively speaking, that has influenced fashion from the 1900s to the present. In their tracks–tracks shaped like those of ballerinas–came the variegated army of the so-called "It Girls", from the precursor Sarah Jessica Parker to Alexa Chung and Olivia Palermo, by way of such heterogeneous icons as Amy Winehouse and Pippa Middleton. Carla Bruni, former First Lady of France, wore them constantly–even on the most official of occasions–perhaps in order not to embarrass her husband, former President Nicolas Sarkozy, more than because of stylistic choice. Perhaps. Some people swear they have even seen Victoria Beckham, heart and soul champion of the stiletto heel, in public only seven millimeters off the ground, the

127 A drawing by Ferragamo shows, with immediacy and elegance, the transition from ballet slippers to ballerina pumps.

129 In *Sabrina* (1954), directed by Billy Wilder, Audrey Hepburn portrayed simple, essential, almost stylized elegance. She is wearing Salvatore Farragamo's flat shoes.

Ballerinas embody the "other woman", the one who is "differently sensual." The one who doesn't need stiletto heels to be enticing.

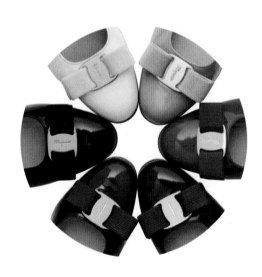

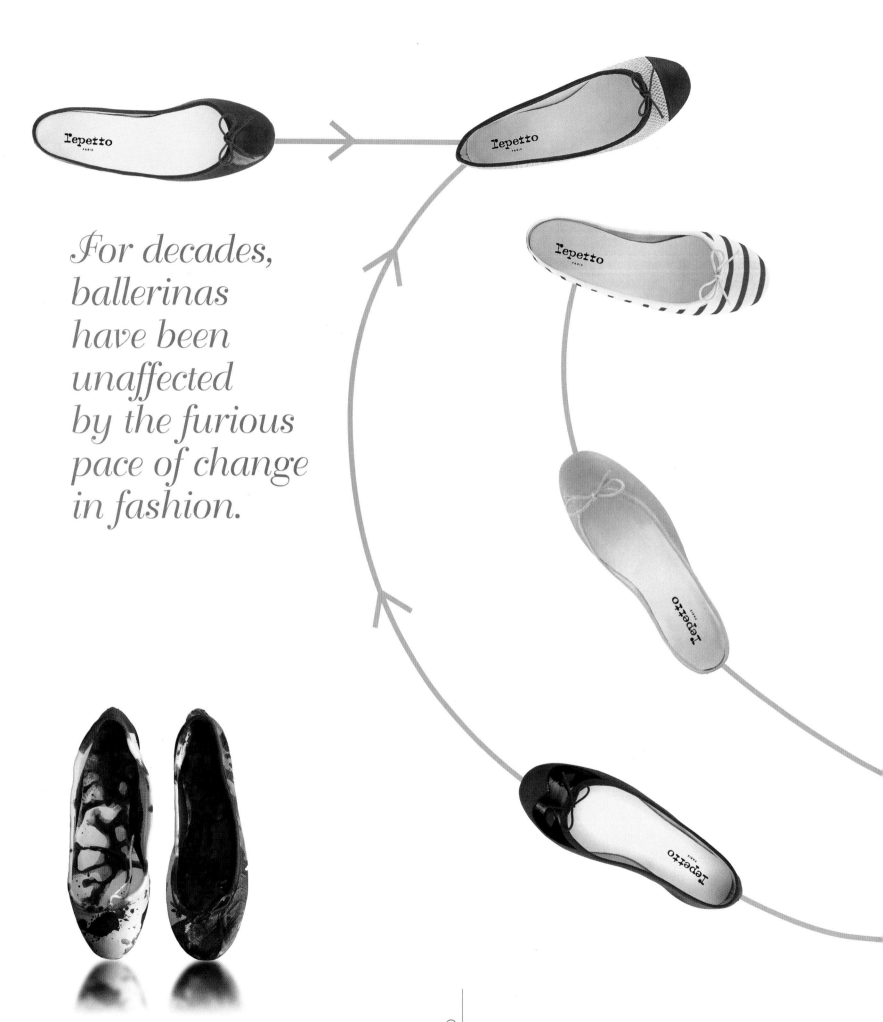

For decades, ballerinas have been unaffected by the furious pace of change in fashion.

If a woman were to have only one pair of shoes they would have to be ballerinas.

typical height of a ballerina heel. Although this news sounds like the usual rumor, it has been confirmed by photographs taken by the paparazzi.

No doubt about it, women love ballerinas. And they have been doing so virtually without interruption since 1956, when an explosive blond bewitched them (in one way, and their husbands in a totally different way) in movie theaters. That blond was Brigitte Bardot, but spectators were so dumbfounded they only managed to babble it. BB was discovered by film director Roger Vadim, who wanted her as the lead in *And God Created Woman* (1956), the orphan Juliette who brought turmoil to an "unknown" fishermen's village, Saint-Tropez. These were clothes that created a myth: red blouse, cream-colored, tight-fitting skirt and black belt that showed off her waist in an unequivocal way. And, on her feet, a pair of flame-red patent leather ballerinas. It was the actress herself who wanted to wear them and asked Maison Repetto for a pair. "I want a pair of shoes for city wear but as comfortable as your ballerina pumps," she must have said. And thus were born Cendrillons.

Since 1947, Milan born, Parisian designer, Rose Repetto, had been creating ballet shoes in her atelier on the Rue de la Paix, not far from the Opéra. She had been encouraged to take up this activity by her son Roland Petit, who at the time was a very young man and who would later become one of the most famous ballet dancers and choreographers of the 20th-century. During the extremely tough classical dance lessons he was taking, Roland was ruining his feet, which often bled due to the exhausting exercises he had to do. His mother, a skilled seamstress, decided to go about designing a pair of ballet shoes for him by adopting the "inside-out" stitch technique, the one used for making gloves, in order to protect his toes as much as possible. Madame Repetto's "ballerina" proved to be such a success that she was induced to undertake a new profession. Repetto ballet shoes were then used by such stars as Maurice Béjart, Rudolf Nureyev, Mikhail Baryshnikov and Carolyn Carlson.

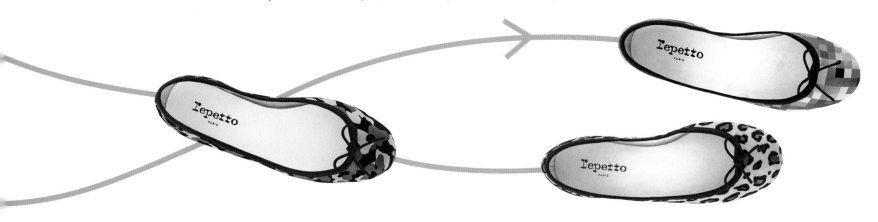

But, if ballerina pumps will never abandon women's feet, credit is due not so much to dancers as to the charm of the slinky Bardot, the "princess of the pout." Beginning with the 1956 Cannes Film Festival, when she was photographed with her red Cendrillons while suavely draped over the hood of a red Simca, ballerinas were a fundamental part of her standard wardrobe, together with capri pants, Vichy canvas dresses, and sweaters with a neckline that generously revealed her shoulders. Women all over the world began to wear ballerinas, imitating both Bardot and another icon of cinema who in that same period also began to wear them quite often: Audrey Hepburn. On the set of *Roman Holiday* (1953) as well as in her daily life, she wore a pair with straps "invented" for her by Salvatore Ferragamo.

Thus, with the "support" of Bardot and Hepburn, ballerinas passed through the decades and were undamaged by the fury of fashion and passing trends. Despite the fierce competition from stiletto and platform heels, wedge and sculptured heels, ballerinas have not disappeared from women's shoe racks. On the contrary. That was because women didn't let themselves be dictated to when it came to shoes. And no one has ever really managed to "liberate" them from their ballerinas.

The question is, why? What was the secret of the apparently invincible and eternal success of those shoes? Was it comfort? Perhaps. But since when has comfort bewitched women? Were they so popular because they went so well with everything? To be honest, one really can't say. The stiletto heel enhances even the most prominent calf and the ballerina requires a well-proportioned figure and slim legs, and even that is not enough sometimes. And so?

Women like ballerinas because they personify and represent the "other woman", the one who is "dif-

ferently sensual." The woman who doesn't need to prove her femininity to anyone; who doesn't try to al-
lure or charm, who doesn't need expedients or stratagems. That woman is more concerned with appreciating herself than with pleasing men; she has a sense of irony and is capable of self-directed irony as well;
she enjoys being a tad gauche; and she smiles if two mice greet her when she puts on a pair of Marc Ja-
cobs cat eye glasses or is approached by a pair of kittens if she has chosen to wear Charlotte Olympia kit-
ty flats. That woman is very chic but also a little bit aloof. She is the other woman who in the collective
imagination is "the Parisian", so magnificently personified and described by the most Parisian muse of all,
Inès de la Fressange–for good reason the muse of Roger Vivier, who added a large metal signature buck-
le to classic ballerinas–in her recently published book, *La Parisienne*. The archetype of a woman that Fressange identifies with the indispensable and irrepressible clothing and accessories in her wardrobe. And,
obviously, ballerinas are entitled to a special place of honor: "If I were to have only one pair of shoes it would
have to be them," the muse said without hesitation. The ballerina fan is a woman who is a little like a child
who doesn't want to grow up, an eternal enthusiast who cultivates her childish side with great elegance
by expressing herself, as sales figures clearly demonstrate, with these "undemanding" shoes.

For that matter, when asked what she wants to be when she grows up, what little girl does not re-
ply: "A ballerina"?

132 Salvatore Ferragamo in 1956, with the "forms" of the feet of the most famous stars in Hollywood and Cinecittà.

133 Repetto has enhanced its collections from season to season with new colors, materials, and details.

134-135 Brigitte Bardot, during a break on the set of *Plucking the Daisy* (1956), wearing those irresistable ballerina pumps.

From K2 to urban chic.

MONCLER 1959

136 The 1959 Moncler logo flirts with the colored graphic of the 1950s and 1960s.

137 The down jacket was created to protect Moncler factory employees from the bitter cold: this picture shows its inevitable shift toward the world of fashion.

The "fatherland" of Moncler is Monestier de Clermont, a mountain village with a few hundred inhabitants not far from Grenoble, in the French Alps. It was there that, in 1952, the enterprising René Ramillon–who had already taken out patents for numerous inventions and had produced metal mountaineering gear that had been used by the French army in World War II–founded his small company, the name of which is an abbreviation of his hometown. He thus began to produce quilted sleeping bags that were highly praised, a single model of a hooded weatherproof jacket and, above all, utilitarian tents with a telescopic structure. The latter were minor masterpieces of functionality and sturdiness that conquered a new generation of vacationers, heirs to a revitalized economy in the immediate postwar period.

But the turning point for Ramillon arrived two years later, in 1954, purely by chance, as was so often the case in the birth of many iconic items that have become milestones in the history of high fashion. In truth, the down jacket had already existed for some time as an item of clothing. The inventor was George Ingle Finch, a mountaineer and chemist who was a pioneer in the development of oxygen masks, which he used in 1922 when he tried to conquer Mt. Everest. But a clumsy jacket literally filled with feathers is one thing, while the Moncler myth, which became a part of the history of high fashion, is quite another.

For the Moncler jacket, the transition from extreme mountaineering to the conquest of the fashion world was brief and inevitable.

The first branded down-filled jackets were produced exclusively to protect Ramillon's factory employees from the bitter cold; they put them over their work overalls. Purely functional, these items were like nylon "boxes" stuffed with goose down, as Ramillon's daughter Annie recalled years later. Although they were prototypes, the first down jackets attracted the attention of an expert in harsh weather conditions: Lionel Terray, a true legend of French mountaineering who conquered 8,000m peaks, the Himalayas, and other giants. On returning from Canada after one of his many epic expeditions, Terray asked Ramillon to create a small collection–a capsule collection, we would call it today, adopting one of the pompous terms that the fashion world invents–of items and accessories specially made to counter extreme cold. Thus was born the "Moncler pour Lionel Terray" line for high-altitude mountaineering: sleeping bags, overalls, jackets and gloves offering optimum protection against the lowest of temperatures. Worn by Terray himself (as well as others), the Moncler collection was the co-protagonist of some heroic missions that marked the basic stages of historic mountaineering feats in the 1950s. In 1954, Moncler "conquered" the summit of K2 by sponsoring the controversial Italian expedition to the top of Karakorum headed by Ardito Desio. The following year Terray led an expedition to the top of Makalu, the fifth highest peak in the world. And again in 1964 Moncler provided Terray with his items for the conquest of the perennial glaciers in Alaska.

140 and 140-141 Prohibitive weather conditions during the Karakorum expedition forced mountaineers to come up with ingenious solutions to the organization of their high-altitude camps. The Moncler down jacket accompanied them during their historic achievement.

Overalls, jackets, and gloves that could provide optimum protection against the cold: the 1950s marked the birth of the Moncler high-altitude mountaineering range.

Colors, volume, details: Moncler changed from season to season, offering stylish models in step with the caprices of fashion.

The transition from extreme mountaineering to sport was short as well as natural. In 1968, Moncler created the official uniform of the French downhill skiing team for the Winter Olympics in Grenoble. Among the many revolutions that shook the world that year, there was one minor one that rejuvenated Ramillon's company. The Moncler logo was changed; the profile of Mt. Eguit, on whose slopes Monestier de Clermont is located, was replaced by a stylized cockerel.

The introduction of the Moncler duvet or quilted jacket to the world of casual apparel was progressive but incessant, thanks to its technical features, which were perfected during this period, and which led to a technological breakthrough with a combination of extraordinary lightness and a unique capacity to retain heat. They were ideal for beginners who went to ski on Sunday and for groups that habitually went on skiing vacations–the numerous enthusiasts of the new winter mass tourism that was growing exponentially. The jackets' light weight was due to their down filling which came from southern Brittany and the Perigord area, where the geese had denser and softer plumage on their stomach and under their wings. In fact, 220 grams of this down was enough to fill a men's blouson and afford 85% insulation. The next stage saw the move from ski runs to city streets; after all, why should the incredible quality and performance of the jackets be restricted to snowy slopes? And so the change came about in the 1980s, culminating in the great success of the cockerel.

After a difficult phase and a change of ownership, during which the Moncler company lost some of its luster, it was taken over by an intelligent and far-sighted entrepreneur from Como, Italy, Remo Ruffini, who purchased it in 2003. His challenging ideas seemed at once both simple and desperate: transform the Moncler duvet into a jacket that could be worn by everybody, everywhere and on all occasions; and even in all seasons. He called this his "global down jacket strategy." This risky venture turned out to be a worldwide success with its innovative materials, its emphasis on stylish items, and its new wearability. Moncler products became a must-have, "exploding" in all directions and greatly influencing the world of high fashion. It had been a long road, from K2 to ski runs, from Piazza San Babila in Milan to the Paris and Milan catwalks that featured the unique Gamme Bleu collection, the sophisticated men's jackets designed by Thom Browne, and the Gamme Rouge deluxe women's collection which was the result of the creativity of a first-class stylist like Giambattista Valli–all in all, truly an achievement for what in 60 years had never contented itself with being a "mere" down jacket.

The introduction of the Moncler duvet jacket into casual wear was gradual but unstoppable. And irreversible.

145 Style icon Sarah Jessica Parker photographed for *Vogue* by Annie Leibovitz.

144

the Chanel Tailleur

The bon ton "uniform" of the contemporary woman.

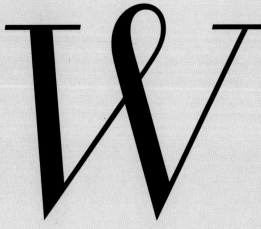

W e are all quite accustomed to the theatrical installations set up by Maison Chanel for its fashion shows. Flamboyant, bombastic backdrops animated by the movements of elegant creatures forged by the pencil of Maison's creative director, Karl Lagerfeld. These are displays of grandeur that Chanel can most certainly brag about. But one more than all others deserves a special place in our collective memory. In January 2008, in the already enchanting setting of the Grand Palais in Paris, King Karl presented Chanel's 2008 spring/summer haute couture collection. Before the show began, journalists, buyers, and celebrities were treated to a grandiose spectacle. An enormous jacket no less that 25 meters high stood precisely under the building's glass dome. It was grey, as if it were made of raw cement, perfect in its proportions and details, absolutely identical to an authentic Chanel jacket. The models–beginning with Sasha Pivovarova–emerged from the slightly open hem of the gigantic jacket, received their portion of admiration and applause, and went back where they had come from, into that magical darkness of the world of fashion unknown to common mortals. The jacket was presented like a totem, like the alpha and omega of the spirit of Chanel, the imaginary place where everything begins and everything ends.

"Every stylist dreams of inventing the Chanel jacket," Lagerfeld admitted. "It is the equivalent of jeans and the T-shirt. Something that is at once neutral, feminine and masculine, as well as the symbol of a timeless fashion." The talented designer's metaphor is as accurate as it is simple. The very essence of the Chanel style, its DNA, its entire story, is contained in the iconic and unmistakable tailleur jacket.

Yes, because the entire creative course of Chanel, with its double C, vacillates between the apparently incompatible extremes that Coco was able to fuse as if by magic: style and functionality, taste and practicability. Her outfit is a prime example of this synthesis. The invention of the woman's suit consisting of a jacket and skirt is attributed to English tailor John Redfern, who supposedly created it way back in 1885. But Coco Chanel deserves full credit and the highest esteem for having revived it in a totally new way in the 1920s. She did away with heavy cloth and stiff lining, which, instead of making women comfortable, only ended up making them feel more ungainly since they were forced to walk with limited and tiring movements. So she opted for jersey fabric, which was "borrowed" from men's underwear and proved to be ideal for making soft and flowing items that

147 1959: a model poses in front of the Paris Chanel boutique.

149 A detail of the light blue tailleur worn by Diana, Princess of Wales, at her son William's confirmation in 1997.
The double C pattern of the buttons is the Chanel "signature."

Nouveau C43

follow body movements. The real turning point arrived in the mid-1950s, when Coco returned to the limelight after a long absence from the catwalks. The deadliest weapon she used to surpass Christian Dior and his growing success was an ensemble of "male" items made of tweed that drew inspiration from Tyrolean jackets worn by the employees of a hotel near Salzburg where she had stayed. Hers was a minor masterpiece of sartorial engineering consisting of the sum of numerous precious and clever technical "maneuvers." The jacket was box-like, and without a collar, with bulky shoulder padding, common at the time. Coco always used to say with conviction: "A garment's elegance lies in the freedom of movement it allows." Thus, no stitching on the chest and only one row in the middle of the back. Then, in order to make it more flexible there was a lateral insert that joined the two parts, making them particularly fluid. The sleeves, cut along the rectilinear grain of the fabric, were sewn directly onto the shoulder and ended in a small slit on the wrist, while a small brass chain was sewn inside the bottom of the hem, and hidden in the lining, to make it hang perfectly. The attached pockets had a purpose that may have been banal but quite useful allowing women to put their hands in them, something not common until that time. All the hems had grosgrain trim of a contrasting color, while special care was taken with the gilded buttons representing lion's heads, camellias or the unmistakable double C. The sheath skirt was knee-length. And the blouse that completed the outfit was the same color as the jacket lining.

"With two black tailleurs and three white blouses–one for the morning, one for the afternoon, and one for the evening–any woman could conquer the world, the heart of the person she loves, and could always be extremely elegant." Mademoiselle was more than certain of the ingeniousness of her creation. The specialist press was a little less certain, at least at the outset. But this should not surprise us, because upsetting the status quo is not the kind of provocation that everyone can understand. However, in this respect women did not have prejudices or preconceived ideas; they grasped the concept right away and immediately accepted the revolutionary nature of that simple suit. It was above all women in the United States–who are second to none when it comes to appreciating comfort–who were instrumental in its success. For the public at large the Chanel tailleurs soon became synonymous with elegance and class, whether they were the expensive originals produced in the Paris atelier on the Rue Cambon or among the more or less faithful imitations that invaded the market. In fact, Coco once admitted: "I would shed tears the day no one copied me."

150 and 151 Karl Lagerfeld, creative director of Maison Chanel since 1983, has never stopped reinterpreting Coco's famous tailleur by using innovative textiles and details, such as sponge and PVC.

Mademoiselle Chanel's revolutionary tailleur is a minor masterpiece of sartorial engineering, consisting of the sum of many precious and clever technical "tricks."

Technically speaking, not even the most ill-fated tailleur in history–the one worn by Jackie Kennedy in Dallas on 22 November 1963, when her husband was assassinated and the course of 20th-century history took a sudden turn–was 100% "Chanel." Presented in Mademoiselle Coco's 1961 autumn/winter collection, the iconic pink outfit with a collar and marine blue details was made from original paper patterns and with Chanel cloth and buttons by Chez Ninon in New York, with permission from Maison Chanel in Paris, a practice that was rather widespread at the time and that in this case made sure the First Lady would not be accused of being a xenophile, given her well-known preference for European glamor.

But, leaving aside the question of authenticity, what strikes one is how the Chanel suit managed to emerge intact from that terrible tragedy, without losing its appeal. Everyone still remembers quite clearly the images of Jackie at Love Field airport next to her husband, the one in which she is on her hands and knees in the limousine, and the other one depicting her as Lyndon B. Johnson was being sworn in as the new president of the United States. What caught our eyes above everything else was the fuchsia stain on the tailleur, so "lurid" and out of place. It is probable that no other outfit has been carved in the collective memory with such violence. No other item of clothing in modern history was fated to be associated with such a terrible tragedy. Jackie's bloodstained suit marked the Western World's loss of innocence and the realization of a much more difficult future.

And yet, despite this, to this day women continue to love it. A true miracle.

152 Actress Anouk Aimée in the Paris Chanel boutique in 1960.

153 A smiling Romy Schneider in the Chanel shop in Rue Cambon. In the background is Mademoiselle Coco, wearing a tailleur very similar to that worn by the Austrian actress.

"With two black tailleurs and three white blouses any woman could conquer the world, the heart of the person she loves, and could always be extremely elegant."

Coco Chanel

154 and 155 A sketch by painter and
illustrator Christian Bérard offers a
vibrant representation of the elegance
of the tailleur and of its creator (right).

157 The Chanel 2012 autumn/winter
collection.

the Chanel Handbag

The shoulder strap bag revolution.

The place of honor that Gabrielle Chanel gained in the history of fashion is the result of one of her inimitable gifts, which indeed may have been a personal shortcoming that the great stylist transformed into her greatest virtue: she considered herself to be the center of the world, a role model for all women, an example, and a pioneer. This was not a question of mythomania, quite the contrary. It was simply that by herself Coco paved the way for a new lifestyle that women in the early 20th-century were not accustomed to but which they felt was already potentially theirs. All Chanel's life was characterized by independence, by freedom and emancipation from pre-conceived rules, by her striking out against hypocrisy and "good manners", which she always questioned and challenged. She offered women–who were aware, as she was, that they could do what they wanted–what would make life easier for them instead of limiting and obstructing them: functionality, feasibility and comfort, for example, which until then had been true taboos of fashion. Coco was the fashion items she designed, because they were the natural outcome of her own needs, which included her dreams. And she knew that her needs were those of a new generation of women. The 2.55, the iconic handbag of Maison Chanel, with its double C, is a perfect example of that flair and that "aesthetic" of hers, which were merged in some way with ethics.

Coco was tired of having to hold her bag in her arms and of losing it, so she added a shoulder strap and carried it on her shoulder, as the stylist herself stated when speaking about the idea that originated her most famous, most loved and most imitated accessory. That was in the 1920s, and Coco was simply unable to understand why women had to have the skills of contortionists and acrobats in order to eat a tidbit, smoke a cigarette, sip a drink and read the libretto of an opera in the theater, since their hands were always occupied with holding their handbags–sophisticated and lovely, to be sure, but terribly uncomfortable–that the fashion of the time had imposed on them on social occasions. We have hands, she must have thought, and so we can surely use them for something more useful or pleasurable than carrying a bag. All that was needed was a shoulder strap, and there you are. She drew inspiration–as she often did and would continue to do–from the world of men's fashion. And she copied the straps on soldiers' saddlebags, adapting them to a small black or dark blue jersey handbag with burgundy or blue grosgrain lining, and created what can be considered the

160 and 161 Jane Fonda, holding her pochette, on the set of *The Game is Over* (1966) directed by her husband Roger Vadim.

The 2.55 is a sort of "patchwork of memory" for Coco.

first thoroughly modern handbag in history. A handbag that, more than an accessory, must be considered an integral part of a woman's attire taken as a whole: no longer far away from the body, thanks to its shoulder strap the new Chanel handbag embraces the body, its curves, becoming one and the same with the rest of the look, which it physically touches and caresses. This handbag is not only used, it is worn, which is a different matter.

This early "sketch" of a handbag was perfected and consecrated 25 years later when, at the age of 71, Mademoiselle–after a long pause during which she was obliged to abstain from participating in fashion shows–made her return more aggressively than ever, determined to combat with pragmatism and common sense the New Look and ultra-feminine woman that Christian Dior had imposed on the immediate postwar period. She responded to the tight waists and wide flared skirts with her revolutionary jersey tailleur, the quintessence of the practicability and relaxed style of the Maison Chanel, an outfit whose worthy complement and accessory could only be a handbag on the same wavelength. The direct heir and natural evolution of the 1929 shoulder strap bag, the 2.55, was officially born in February 1955. Its name corresponds to the date of its appearance. It had no frills, no allusions, and no superfluous embellishments. Coco went straight to the essence of things. Even in the most iconic handbag–and this is another of the extraordinary gifts that made Mademoiselle Chanel great–the stylist inserted more or less private fragments of her life, her memories and habits, even her nightmares. The 2.55 is a sort of "patchwork of memory" for Coco, a moving, sentimental Frankenstein.

The skin used for the handbag, plongé or dipped lambskin or calfskin, is made softer and is lent greater consistency through the matelassé or quilted diamond-shaped pattern. This was inspired by the jackets worn by jockeys that the stylist had observed on so many occasions at the racetracks she frequented. The inner lining is a bright burgundy that tends toward brown, the same color of the uniforms that Coco, like all other children, had had to wear during those sad years she spent in the orphanage at Aubazine. "I know women," she later said. "Give them chains, women adore chains." But her choice of a chain to be used as the handbag strap was not as banal and obvious as it may seem: it was the double chain that she "borrowed" from the custodians of her orphanage, who had used it to keep their keys attached to their waists. On the back side of the bag was a handy small outer pocket for banknotes, which also offered women more independence in that they could have and spend money when and how they wished. Another pocket inside the front flap was zippered; rumor had it that it was here that Coco kept by her side, but always hidden from indiscreet eyes, her love letters. The very simple gilded front lock was called the Mademoiselle Lock, alluding to the fact that Coco had never married.

Like all Coco's extraordinary inventions, the 2.55 survived the death of its creator, which occurred in 1971. This was due, for the most part, to Karl Lagerfeld, who, since 1983, has been the creative director of Maison Chanel and who, collection after collection, set out to embellish, enhance and alter the bag that in the meantime had become a cult object.

162 and 163 The inside lining of the 2.55 is bright burgundy and there
is a pocket flap with a zipper.

"I know women; give them chains, women adore chains."

Coco Chanel

He did this at times with the amazing inspiration that only he possesses, at other times with respect that smacks of absolute devotion, such as the time in the mid-1980s when he began to delicately restyle the bag with minimal but substantial alterations while creating the famous classic flaps. In the rings of the double-chain strap he inserted a strip of leather, and he replaced the Mademoiselle Lock with the Double C Lock with its interwoven double C that, in this period of what could be called logomania, has spread like an epidemic among followers of fashion. These "classic flaps" were a great success but did not eclipse the popularity of the original model: on the contrary, in February 2005, the 50th anniversary of the 2.55 witnessed the presentation of a bag that was absolutely identical to the prototype, down to the tiniest detail. The 2.55 has remained true to itself and even today its creation takes ten hours of work by six artisans who assemble its 180 parts by hand.

While women may have changed, their needs certainly have not. To this day they have "a desperate need for Chanel," as fashion editor Nigel says to awkward Andrea in *The Devil Wears Prada* (2006).

Ray-Ban & PerSol

From heroic aviators to Hollywood stars.

The Aviator is the symbol of the vital, carefree, cheeky, and yet seductive spirit of the United States.

Two similar stories, two parallel roads. A curious series of analogies and coincidences in the past, and a present that in many respects is overlapping, the only difference being the contexts and, in a certain sense, the "proportions." Ray-Ban and Persol originated in places that could not be more different. But today they are linked because they are favorites of the "greats" in movies, music, and fashion who want to protect their eyes from the sun and/or conceal their eyes and glances from the ubiquitous paparazzi. Or only–and more probably–to create an enigmatic, mysterious air around their persona with a mere pair of sunglasses that may cover what are considered to be the "mirrors of the soul" but that paradoxically reveal the soul of those wearing them much more than any other accessory is able to do.

Both brands were created in response to a technical need, and soon specialized in the production of glasses made to meet the needs of aviators. However, both would develop, in parallel, a program of technological improvement and stylistic research, thus attracting greater and greater numbers of fans and admirers. Both represent the characteristics of the countries in which they were created. While Ray-Ban epitomizes the vital, vigorous, carefree, cheeky and yet seductive spirit of the United States, Persol represents the most authentic Italian taste, its cunning elegance, Italy's intellectual and adorably impertinent character. Lastly, both brands are now in the designer label portfolio of Luxottica, a fashion eyewear company, headed by the Italian Leonardo Del Vecchio, that contends for leadership in the sphere of the most popular and best-selling sunglasses in the world.

The creator of the legendary Ray-Ban is Bausch & Lomb–an American optical company located in Rochester, New York whose traditions hark back to 1853– which, on 7 May 1937, registered a patent for Anti-Glare, which would make its fortune. This was the most epic period in the history of aviation, when flights were becoming longer, more and more complicated and fatiguing, and pilots were true heroes. Many of them, when approaching the Sun, like Icarus, were subject to annoying disturbances. While the wax wings of the mythical son of Daedalus melted, pilots in the 1920s and 1930s suffered from dizziness and intense headaches. The reason for this was the strong glare of

the sun. Anti-Glare sunglasses, with their very light frames, originally made of plastic and later of gilded metal, had lenses made of mineral glass able to filter out ultraviolet and infrared rays without lessening visual acuity and definition.

The original "banish rays" glasses became highly popular under the abbreviated name Ray-Ban. The US Air Force officially adopted Ray-Ban Aviators as part of its equipment, and civilians also began to wear them. They wore Ray-Bans to protect their eyes from the reflections in the water while fishing or from the noonday sun while hunting. Their growing popularity was accompanied by constant technological improvements. During World War II Ray-Ban conceived the gradient mirror lens, which made the performance of the Aviator model more sophisticated, because pilots could now clearly see their instrument panels. They were also worn by General Douglas MacArthur, C-in-C Allied Forces in the South Pacific, upon his arrival in the Philippine Islands. The photographs of his landing there were seen in newspapers all over the world, and MacArthur involuntarily advertised the teardrop-shaped sunglasses that everyone now wanted as an emblem of the most authentic American spirit, with all its evident potential for glamor. Their monopoly on public approval was challenged only in 1952, when Ray-Ban came out with another highly successful model, the Wayfarer. While the earlier model had been very lightweight and fragile-looking, the later one, with its plastic frame and Raymond Stegeman's revolutionary design, gave the impression of solidity, security, and fascination, as well as a touch of irony that, until then, had been lacking in sunglasses. Michael Jackson and Tom Cruise were identified with the Ray-Ban Aviator. The latter lent a new, worldwide popularity to this model by wearing it in the hugely successful *Top Gun* (1986), in which he portrayed an adventurous and heroic pilot–what else?

169 Tom Cruise's portrayal of Lieutenant Pete "Maverick" Mitchell in *Top Gun*
(1986) directed by Tony Scott, turned him into a star.

Although lightweight and fragile-looking, the famous teardrop-shaped sunglasses exude a vigorous character that alludes to their military origin.

172 Douglas MacArthur, C-in-C Allied Forces in the South Pacific, also wore the famous brand. This kind of endorsement transformed them from a mere accessory into a cult "must-have."

173 This 1940s ad reveals the close relationship between the Aviator model and the world of military aviation.

174-175 The undeniable glamour attached to these sunglasses made them a favorite among stars of the entertainment world, including Robert Redford (left), and The Who's drummer Keith Moon (right).

THE WORLD'S FINEST SUNGLASSES

Why should you pay more for Ray-Ban Sun Glasses? (They sell from $8.95 to $24.95). The answer is that your eyes deserve the protection they get *only* from sun glasses made of genuine optical glass, ground-and-polished-to-curve. Especially when you drive...you'll appreciate the way Ray-Ban lenses protect your eyes from dazzling sunlight, filter out the harmful rays as no ordinary sun glass can. Safe drivers, like jet pilots, know the eye-saving, life-saving value of Ray-Ban Sun Glasses. Choose from Neutral Gray G-15, Ray-Ban Green or Gradient Density lenses, all three in your choice of over 70 frame styles and colors — superbly crafted to last a rugged lifetime. For full enjoyment under the sun get Ray-Ban...the most distinguished name in Sun Glasses. Look for the name on the frame. In optical offices and fine stores. Bausch & Lomb Incorporated, Rochester, N.Y.

TRY ON A PAIR—YOU WON'T SETTLE FOR LESS!

"Signet"

"Vagabond"

BAUSCH & LOMB

Ray-Ban ®

SUN GLASSES

Your prescription? Available in *any* of the smart Ray-Ban frames, or in conventional eyewear styles.

There is no Hollywood star who doesn't become more fascinating thanks to a pair of teardrop-shaped sunglasses.

The pride and joy of Italian creativity, inventiveness and excellence are the Persol sunglasses. Behind the success of this world-famous brand stands an entrepreneur from Piedmont, Italy, who was a photographer and owner of Berry's opticians, which in 1917, in a courtyard on Via Caboto in Turin, began to make avant-garde sunglasses expressly for early aviators and intrepid sports pilots. The Protector model, which had a rubber frame and round lens, was used by the Italian armed forces and air force. Among the most enthusiastic fans of the Piedmontese label was Gabriele D'Annunzio, who wore them—not as a poet but as a major—during an historic flight over Vienna in 1918, during which he dropped thousands of patriotic leaflets. But it was in 1938 that the Persol trademark proper was created. As its name suggests (it is the abbreviation of per il sole, or "for the sun"), it was designed to protect wearers from the sun's rays. The period was marked by two technical innovations that will always be proudly worn on the chest of the Persol label much like a soldier's medals. The first is Meflecto, a futuristic system that introduced flexible, and virtually unbreakable, frame wings. The second is the iconic Freccia or arrow—the hinge on the frame wing decorated with an arrow whose shape drew inspiration from ancient warriors' swords—which was to become one of the unmistakable (and frequently copied) details of the Persol style.

But the turning point for the small company was 1957 thanks to the 649 model. Conceived to help tram drivers in Turin, who were at the mercy of the wind, air, and dust because their drivers' seats were still exposed to the elements, the Persol 649, with its unmistakable yellow-brownish lens, covered a large area and protected both the eyes and part of the face from sunlight, and at the same time added a touch of Latin charm and glamor. That is the reason why, among a host of international stars who have worn them, from Greta Garbo to Steve McQueen, the most memorable is Marcello Mastroianni in *Divorce Italian Style* (1961).

178-179 In addition to its technical innovations, the PO714SM model exudes a rather cunning and intellectual elegance, features that were interpreted perfectly by Steve McQueen.

Kelly & Birkin

Two names, a single desire.

*T*he birth of a legend is often wrapped in mystery and obscurity, as it should be. And this is also the case with what has been universally considered to be the most iconic handbag for over 50 years. Known the world over by its nickname, the Hermès Kelly.

We are not absolutely certain when this product was "born." In the 1930s Robert Dumas, a fourth-generation Parisian leather-goods manufacturer specializing in saddlery and travel goods, created the "petit sac de voyage à courroie, pour dames." As its explanatory but not so appealing name tells us, this was a woman's trapezoidal handbag with a double strap clasp and a small padlock for security. It was a direct descendant of one of the most popular Hermès handbags, the large and extremely comfortable Haut à Courroies, created at the end of the 19th-century by Émile-Maurice Hermès to meet the needs of the newborn "hyperkinetic man" who, thanks to new means of transport–the automobile–discovered an indispensable ally and companion for his explorations of the world, both long and short. While the Haut à Courroies was specially designed for jockeys and horsemen, who could use it to carry their saddlery while riding in their cars to new racing and riding adventures, the petit sac of the 1930s was designed for women and their new lifestyle, which had become more dynamic, enterprising, free, and autonomous. The handbag was similar in shape and character to its "ancestor", but was much smaller. With only one strap, it was designed so that women could carry it around comfortably in their hands. It had four metal "feet" riveted to the bottom and could thus be placed anywhere, even on the ground, unlike other "respectable" handbags that were then in vogue.

But when, precisely, in the history of luxury leather goods, this iconic bag was named after American actress Grace Kelly, Academy Award winner for *The Country Girl* (1954) and muse of Alfred Hitchcock, is still a mystery. Some people have claimed that the legendary, coveted bag became highly popular and the object of almost hysterical collective yearning in 1956, when a photograph appeared in *Life Magazine* showing the actress, accompanied by her husband Prince Rainier III of Monaco, covering her stomach from the curious eyes and cameras of the paparazzi with one of the many Hermès handbags in her collection, in an attempt to keep her pregnancy a secret.

181 Grace Kelly and Prince Rainier of Monaco in January 1956: the royal couple, immortalized, on the day of their official engagement.

The Kelly Bag is the ancestor of "It Bags", but it surpasses them all, occupying a special place among 20th-century accessories.

However, it's a pity that there is no trace of this photograph in *Life Magazine's* archives. So, is it an urban legend or not? We know that every myth contains a basic truth and has some relationship to reality, and this seems to be no exception. Because there is one certain fact: the photographs of the official engagement of Grace Kelly and Prince Rainer, in her parents' home in Pennsylvania, in early January 1956, were seen all over the world. And it is also certain that the outfit she chose to wear on that important occasion, a white dress with tiny *ton sur ton* patterns and a flared skirt, was accompanied by the iconic bag. It is possible, if not probable, that the public relationship between the cold, steely actress and the practical accessory began precisely on that occasion and that it was then spontaneously and constantly fostered by her many public appearances on the arm of Prince Rainier–even when she was expecting her first child, Caroline. And this persuaded Hermès to officially adopt the nickname "Kelly" for the bag, which in the meantime had become all the rage.

Grace Kelly was also involved in the origin of the phenomenon of the so-called "It Bags", the icon that every conscientious fashion lover–provided she could afford it–should have in her collection, which should be enlarged with new items every season, much to the joy of the fashion industry. But while the ones produced today are must-haves created in keeping with rigorous marketing strategies, the one dedicated to Princess Grace began in a totally natural way.

184 and 185 A mini Kelly Bag in iconic orange and a version in shearling, presented at the Hermès 2010-2011 autumn/winter show. These are only a few of the Bag's entertaining interpretations.

And if this holds true for Kelly, it is even more so for the Birkin, the second Hermès handbag to become part of the pantheon of the fashion-addicted all over the world. That bag was also known by a simple family name. Its history began with a random circumstance, a chance meeting. And this time there is no mystery or doubt, since the story was narrated by the person directly involved. One day in 1983, Jane Birkin and Jean-Louis Dumas met during a flight from Paris to London. She was the beautiful English actress and singer who had become famous in Michelangelo Antonioni's *Blow Up* (1966) and also thanks to her sultry sighs in the scandalous "Je t'aime... moi non plus", which she recorded with her partner Serge Gainsbourg. Dumas had been chief executive of Hermès since 1978. Before takeoff, Birkin had tried to put her bag in the airplane's overhead lockers. But a young mother like herself certainly does not travel with an "essential" handbag. Her crammed bag fell and the contents spilled all over the floor. Even the notes, pieces of paper and documents in her Hermès diary went flying. Since she was seated next to Dumas, Birkin did not miss the opportunity to utter a couple of "complaints": besides a bag with pockets, she wanted one so capacious that it could contain the thousand indispensable objects (and the thousand superfluous ones) that every woman always wants to have close at hand. No sooner said than done. Dumas set about creating one to suit her needs. But while it is not complicated to add pockets to diaries (a feature that has remained), creating the "perfect bag" was quite another story. However, Dumas understood that no magic tricks were necessary since the answer was already part and parcel of the Hermès tradition of which he was then in charge. Once again it was the Haut à Courroies, by then almost a century old, that provided a solution; extremely supple, a small reduction in its size made the new bag almost perfect for the "uncontrollable" needs of modern women. Jane Birkin liked the new bag and the two became inseparable companions and thus she became the new bag's "letter of recommendation", as well as its inspiration. That is, until the moment, 25 years later, when tendonitis forced her to choose accessories that were perhaps less iconic but lighter. In 2011 she abandoned the Birkin 1 model and was taken by the fascination of a small bag with a Scottish tartean pattern. Her legendary black bag was auctioned off for more than 110,000 Euros, which went to charity.

187 Jane Birkin (right), with "her" cult bag and a detail of the Birkin Bag closure (above).

188 and 189 Two phases in the long and painstaking hand-crafted production of the bag. To guarantee perfection it takes between 18 and 24 hours to make each bag.

It is neither a mystery nor a surprise that both these handbags are a permanent fixture in the pantheon of women's desires. And the reason for this is that in this period of technical reproduction and mass and global production, the Kelly and Birkin bags have jealously preserved the magnificent "imperfection" that their rigorously handcrafted creation entails. It takes between 18 and 24 hours to make each bag by hand, and this delicate and painstaking work is done by expert artisans who are able to join the dozens of components by means of thousands of inimitable saddle stitches. Both models can be custom-made to fit the needs of even the most discerning clientele; the variety of precious skins available upon request and the range of sizes and colors make for possible combinations that are virtually infinite. Yet, despite the prices, which have three or even four zeros, there are waiting lists for both these handbags. It is not enough to want a Hermès bag and to be able to afford one. You must also have the right credentials, so to speak, to be "worthy" of one, as well as a lot of patience, before being able to enjoy it. Despite this, there are women who collect both models in a determined and near-maniacal way: Victoria Beckham seems to have at least one hundred of them.

Over the years, both the Kelly and the Birkin bags have undergone imaginative and surprising varia-

tions and alterations thanks to the genius of the stylists in this great fashion house, from Martin Margiela to Jean-Paul Gaultier. One can admire, on the catwalks, the passage of the supple and "foldable" Kelly Flat and Kelly Relax models, as well as the Shoulder model, the Wicker, and the Ado, a backpack version, while the Shadow version of the Birkin bag, with its trompe l'oeil effect, has been very successful. Finally, on the sidewalk one will often find originals outnumbered by bad imitations of both. In fact, the Kelly and the Birkin certainly compete as the most imitated and forged handbags in the history of fashion. And this is also an important sign of their success. As English author Charles Caleb Colton once declared, "Imitation is the sincerest form of flattery."

Kelly and Birkin Bags retain an "imperfection" that manual production entails.

Little BlaCK DrEsS

The infinitely elegant little dress.

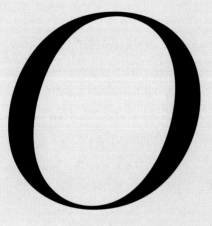

One of the unwritten tenets of the imaginary fashion code has it that even the most naïve, unsophisticated woman, when asked to give an opinion about style and elegance, will enthusiastically agree that the little black dress (LBD) is one of the items that must be part of a woman's wardrobe. This was confirmed by a survey–conducted in 2007 and promoted by the Clothes Show broadcast on the British TV channel "UKTV Style"–of 3,000 women viewers, and published in *The Daily Mail*, a popular tabloid newspaper. When asked to name the most important item in the history of women's fashion, British women did not hesitate. 96% responded, and of those 76% named the LBD. Another survey, this time by *The Independent* newspaper, noted women's extraordinary appreciation of the LBD: 96% of those interviewed had at least one, 48% had more than one, and–no surprise here–54% of men respondents declared they would like to have their woman wear one.

Authority was conferred on these pithy statistics by master fashion designer, Karl Lagerfeld, who stated: "One is never over-dressed or underdressed with a Little Black Dress." Donna Karan, who knows all about powerful women, gave an ideal nod of approval: "The little black dress is the foundation of every woman's wardrobe." The late and never sufficiently lamented Alexander McQueen laid it on even thicker when he said that "it's the embodiment of female power: raw, frank and straight to the point." An opinion confirmed by another fashion giant, Christian Dior, who commented on the timeless fascination of this cult dress as follows: "You can wear black at any time. You can wear it at any age. You may wear it to almost any occasion. A little black frock is essential to a woman's wardrobe." And if these personages say it, we can–or rather, we must–believe it.

For that matter, the affection women all over the world have for this item is a fact that, all things considered, is easy to explain. Nothing like the little black dress is at once so rigorous and yet so versatile. And it makes women seem a little slimmer, which is always something that is greatly appreciated. Different, often very heterogeneous, styles and lines can co-exist in this macro-category. The gamut of LBDs ranges from the monastic to the super sexy because, as the generality of its very definition prescribes, an LBD, in order to be such, must respect three simple preconditions: it must be a dress, be black, and be

193 Audrey Hepburn on the set of *Breakfast at Tiffany's* (1961): birth of a legend.

"little." The little black dress is an idea around which one can invent one's own look, making it to order. And this was, and still is, the formula for its popularity.

The first person to discover this "secret" was the ingenious Gabrielle Chanel, a person who was second to none as far as understanding what women really needed. When, way back in 1926, she designed the silhouette of the first *petite robe noir* of the modern age, Mademoiselle Coco sparked an explosive cultural and aesthetic revolution. And not so much, or not only, because she revived and consigned to women's everyday life a color that until then had been used exclusively in mourning or by priests or maids, but because she created a wholly new "uniform" with which women could face modern life, a dress that made them feel more confident, independent, and aggressive because they were more comfortable and more at their ease. Frills do not impart style, nor do useless details bestow respectability. In a world that seemed to be custom-built for men only, women had to focus on the concrete, not the superfluous. With caustic irony and ill-concealed immodesty, Coco, commenting on her creation, stated that women dressed poorly and that she had pulled a fast one on them all with her black dress so that they would learn to have some taste. She treated women rather badly, but only because she sincerely loved them.

According to popular legend, it took her only an hour and a half to draw her revolutionary creation one boring afternoon. And, whether she was inspired by grief over the loss of her great love and mentor, Arthur "Boy" Capel, who died in an automobile accident in 1919 or whether her invention was an oblique, *sui generis* tribute to the attire of the teachers and nuns in the Congregation of the Sacred Heart at Aubazine, the orphanage where she and her sisters were sent when very young, makes very little difference. These are details that only a Freud might have been interested in. Chanel's first LBD was made of silk crepe; it was calf-length, had long sleeves and a crew neck, and its decoration consisted of light *ton sur ton* diagonal lines. No buttons, no embroidery, no frills. It was worn with hair of a boyish cut, a cloche hat and a string of pearls, the embodiment of Coco Chanel's mantra: "Every day I simplify something because every day I learn something." *Vogue America*, the official gazette of fashion trends, published an illustration of the LBD in the form of a sketch in its November issue, describing it with words that would be associated with the dress forever: "For any girl, any woman with little money, it's marvelous to have the possibility of having one dress for the whole season, for the whole year, and be well dressed." And even for a whole life, if you want. As simple as it was audacious, the little black dress scandalized and persuaded at the same time. Vogue nicknamed it "Chanel's Ford"–a reference to the popularity and accessibility of the mass-produced automobile and a recognition of the LBD's potential to equal such suc-

cess ("the dress the whole world will wear"). Others, less far-sighted, were bewildered and upset, and reacted with such statements as "fashion for little, undernourished telegraph operators." It was history and women who proved Coco right.

Reinvented continuously in the following decades, the little black dress was transformed while remaining faithful to itself, and while being worn by half the world's women. The LBD worn by cartoon character Betty Boop was short and scandalous, with her garters fully exposed; Elsa Schiaparelli's had impressive shoulders; Wallis Simpson's was austere. For Edith Piaf it was a sort of uniform. Then, in the 1950s, came Christian Dior's New Look. And Marilyn Monroe's LBD was sinuous, enhancing her figure even in two-dimensional black-and-white photographs in magazines.

But popularity is one thing and legend is quite another. And the LBD would not be the icon it is if the long model designed by Hubert de Givenchy had not been worn by a unique person in a movie–that elf of elegance and femininity named Audrey Hepburn in *Breakfast at Tiffany's* (1961), based on a book by Truman Capote and directed by Blake Edwards. The opening scene goes as follows. On a deserted Fifth Avenue in New York City, the female lead, Holly Golightly, gets out of a taxi, stops in front of the shop windows of a famous jeweler's while nibbling on a pastry and drinking coffee. She is wearing large sunglasses, a small crown on her gathered up hair, long black gloves, and a cascade of pearls flowing over her shoulder blades. And a long black dress that obliges her to walk with tiny steps. Givenchy had intended the dress to have a slit, but due to "cinematographic requirements" the famous costume designer Edith Head transformed it into an authentic sheath dress. Thus was born the myth that bewitched millions of women. And thus was born a heroine that generations of girls identified with and emulated. And what does it matter if the dress in that opening scene was, technically speaking, an evening dress? Nor does it matter that the real LBD of this cult movie is another one, worn in a later scene, knee-length and accompanied by a wide-brimmed hat. What is historical accuracy compared to the utter enchantment of myth? A mere detail.

196 and 197 Audrey Hepburn on the set of *Breakfast at Tiffany's* (1961), wearing one of two black dresses specially designed for her by Hubert de Givenchy (right).

brunetta 1949

"*Women dress poorly and I pull a fast one on them all with my black so that they will learn to have some taste.*"

Coco Chanel

198 The interpretation of the Chanel LBD by the mythical illustrator Brunetta (Bruna Mateldi Moretti).

199 Sexy, even if two-dimensional. Betty Boop "seduced" men in the 1930s by revealing her garters, which seemed to emerge from beneath her short V-neckline dress.

the JACKie Bag

The unforgettable handbag of an inimitable icon.

The eclectic Michelle Obama and the hyper *bon ton* Carla Bruni Sarkozy can set their minds at rest. The most stylish First Lady in modern times was (and still is) Jackie Kennedy. Or, more simply, Jackie. During the years she lived in the White House with her husband John F. Kennedy, whom she married in 1953 and who died tragically in Dallas in 1963, Jackie enchanted the United States and the whole world with her colored sheaths and essential evening dresses designed by Oleg Cassini, delicately enhanced by a precious jewel that was not gaudy. But what is even more radical, she imposed her personal but imitable and much imitated style on the whole world when she added to her first husband's name that of Aristotle Onassis, the Greek shipping magnate who, in 1968, became her second husband. And it was precisely in the period bridging the second half of the 1960s and the early 1970s that saw the most innovative and incisive Jackie, from a stylistic standpoint, the person everyone calls Jackie O. The one who set aside her three strings of pearls and Chanel tailleurs and began to wear jeans or capri pants, and concealed her glance–sad or combative–behind enormous sunglasses. The Jackie who walked barefoot in the harbor on the island of Skorpios and who squeezed into a trench coat with the collar turned up. The one who abandoned the iconic haircut that Kenneth Batelle had conceived for her in favor of a silk scarf wrapped around her head with modern hippie-chic taste.

Thus liberated from her institutional role–which, it must be said, she never "endured" but, on the contrary, was very fond of–Jackie became the icon of a hyper-contemporary and metropolitan style that favored rather loose-fitting and dynamic daywear over striking evening wear. A style depicted almost obsessively by the father of American paparazzi, Ron Galella, who immortalized her in hundreds of photographs taken, on the sly, on the streets of New York. The photographer's constant

203 Jackie Kennedy on a New York City street: an integral part of her dynamic contemporary look was the Jackie Bag.

204 Jackie Kennedy and John Jr. during a vacation spent on the island of Ischia: by her side is her Jackie Bag.

The accessory that identified and epitomized an entire aesthetic: the calling card of the "Jackie style."

stalking angered and frustrated the former First Lady, who took him to court and obtained a restraining order that obliged him to stay at least 50 feet away from her. But we, who to this day admire her innate class, must admit that these photographs have allowed us to fully understand the power and fascination of her outfits, an almost constant integral part of which was a shoulder bag that at the time began to be universally known as the Jackie bag. This is a bag that, were it a rhetorical figure of speech, would be called a synecdoche: the part that stands for the whole, the accessory that epitomizes an entire aesthetic. In other words, the calling card of the "Jackie style." As is the case with the equally legendary Hermès Kelly bag, this was a bag that had been in the Gucci catalog for years but that was brought into the limelight–and in a certain sense immortalized–only when an icon of fashion began to wear it as if she could not bear being without it and was thus "doomed" to have her name linked to it.

When Gucci launched the bag in 1958, it had the rather anonymous name of G1097. An alphanumeric name seemed to be appropriate for an accessory that no one would ever have imagined, in a few years' time, would become one of most popular bags in the world. The trapezoidal shape of the bag, manufactured by this famous Florentine designer label, drew inspiration from the feeder that hangs from horses' necks. A shape that is therefore in keeping with the equestrian image typical of this luxury-goods manufacturer, which has made stirrups and bridles the hallmarks of its most identifiable trademark. The original bag was made of printed fabric with Renaissance dec-

206 The Jackie Bag in iconic canvas with GG logo.

oration, details in red leather and a snap closure. In 1961 it was modified and "corrected"; the well-known push lock closure was introduced with the G1244 model. The key to the success of the Jackie bag was, probably, also what superficially might seem to have been its fundamental limit. The Jackie bag popularized the concept of the "everyday bag", adapted to all looks, and was even considered as "a bag for life." Unlike the custom at the time, the Jackie bag was not a handbag connected to a particular context or occasion. With its rounded corners, few details, innate "understatement" and overall appeal, the Jackie bag would not overwhelm any personal style with an overly obtrusive personality, but on the contrary could be adapted to any outfit thanks to its flexibility. The Jackie bag is almost the archetype of the modern handbag, the one that accompanies a woman all day long, capacious but not cumbersome, eclectic but not capricious. It is the bag handed down from mother to daughter, as Jackie's daughter, Caroline Kennedy, demonstrated by wearing it frequently when she turned twenty and tried to emulate her mother's style, which may have been a little overpowering.

The Jackie bag has become part of the 21st-century without showing its age. But it did undergo significant restyling just after celebrating its 50th birthday in splendid shape. That was in 2009, when Gucci creative director Frida Giannini launched the New Jackie. The company's new cult bag with its double "G" is faithful to the spirit of the original but with a "contemporary flair", and immediately enjoyed great success. Its proportions have been somewhat modified and it is slightly more ca-

207 The unmistakable floral print handbag alternates with the traditional
Gucci logo in the hearts of aficionados of this inimitable classic.

pacious, while what the company called its "deconstructed form" lent it a new softness. The details have acquired more character; these include the large leather topstitching and the leather tassels with finished bamboo inserts, a distinctive material used by that designer label. Luxury, in the most modern sense of the term, is what characterizes this bag, thanks to the use of fine skins such as crocodile and python and the painstaking and precious skill of expert Italian craftsmen. And the fact that Gucci has decided to call this new bag simply the "New Jackie" must mean something, perhaps that there is no longer a woman whose taste is comparable to that of the legendary Jackie? This is also a sign of the times, when all is said and done.

208 and 209 Long leather tassels, bamboo inserts and a soft, deconstructed form:
this is the most modern interpretation of a timeless classic.

the STILETTO

Sensuality on women's feet.

We could spend a lot of time trying to establish who invented the stiletto heel and would come up with only one certainty–that we will never find an exhaustive, definitive answer shared by all alike. If the custom of wearing shoes that raise men and women above the ground is lost in the mists of time–supposedly as long ago as 3500 BC ancient Egyptian butchers used high heels in order not to dirty their feet with blood in the slaughterhouses, and Mongol horsemen used them to have their feet placed more firmly in the stirrups–then it is impossible to attribute with any degree of certainty who created the thin, high heel with the smallest of bases that has revolutionized the history of fashion and changed the very concept of femininity.

According to legend, Caterina de' Medici, on the occasion of her wedding to the Duke of Orléans in 1533, wore high heels in order to compensate for her short stature. It seems that an equally vain woman, Mary Tudor, consort to the king of France, couldn't do without them. Even Marie Antoniette supposedly appeared before the guillotine in 1793 wearing heels nine centimeters high. But the bold designs of the modern shoe-making industry, which are related to physics and engineering, have very little, or nothing, to do with the aristocratic sculptures of these–and so many other–noblewomen. The stiletto heel was created solely with the idea of replacing the delicate and fragile wood with a very thin but highly resistant metal core inside the heel so that it could become thinner and taller than anyone could ever have dreamt of.

Many people attribute the origin of the stiletto heel to Italian-born French shoemaker André Perugia, who in the 1920s "elevated" women–such as the popular French singer Mistinguett, a harbinger of the stiletto–to vertiginous heights. Others grant the honor of having conceived the metallic inner structure of heels to the underrated stylist Kristin S. Wagner. But almost everyone agrees that the 1950s was the decade when, partly thanks to movie stars, stiletto heels became a mainstay of women's fashion. Marilyn Monroe–who, despite what is commonly believed, was definitely not a dumb blond–once declared in defense of high-heels: "I don't know who invented high heels, but all women owe him a lot." Fashion historians also disagree as to which designer label was the true promoter of the stiletto boom. Many award the medal for having invented this heel to Frenchman Roger Vivier, who worked side by side with Chris-

211 Shoe designer Manolo gained world fame because of the obsessive admiration of his shoes by Sarah Jessica Parker's character Carrie Bradshaw, in *Sex and the City*.

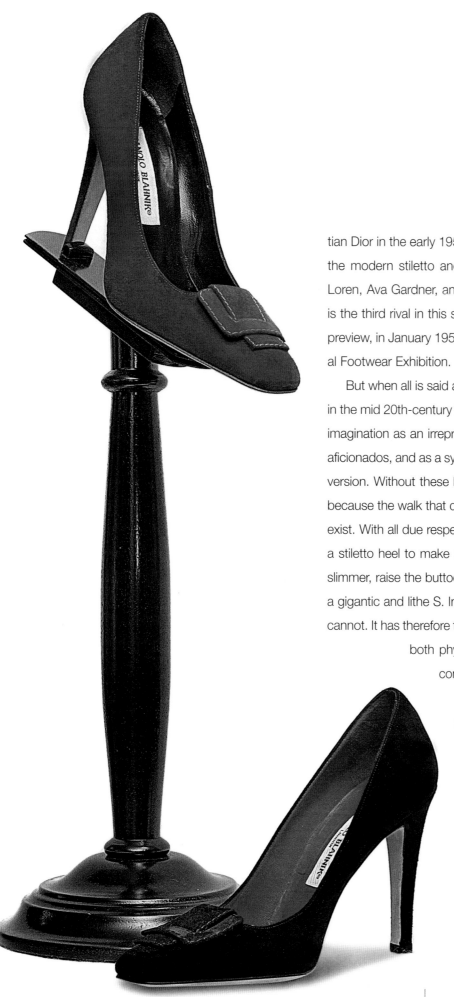

tian Dior in the early 1950s. But many others believe that Salvatore Ferragamo created the modern stiletto and made it popular using such famous feet as those of Sofia Loren, Ava Gardner, and Greta Garbo. The small town of Vigevano in Lombardy, Italy is the third rival in this struggle among fashion giants, since it hosted the official world preview, in January 1953, of the first stiletto heel on the occasion of the XVI International Footwear Exhibition.

But when all is said and done, what does it matter? What we know for certain is that in the mid 20th-century the stiletto heel made its spectacular entrance into the collective imagination as an irrepressible means of seduction, as a cult object worshipped by its aficionados, and as a symbol of sensual femininity that is delicate but with a dash of perversion. Without these heels, femmes fatales, sex symbols, and stars would not exist, because the walk that distinguishes a regular woman from a sensual woman would not exist. With all due respect to orthopedic surgeons and physiatrists, there is nothing like a stiletto heel to make a leg seem more slender, make the calf taper, make the ankle slimmer, raise the buttocks and arch the natural curves of the body, transforming it into a gigantic and lithe S. In other words, the stiletto can do what aesthetic plastic surgery cannot. It has therefore transcended its primary function of increasing a woman's height, both physically and optically, and has invaded a field that is intimately connected with desire, voluptuousness and even eroticism.

The person who reinvented the stiletto heel in an original and unique way, in the mid 1970s, was a designer from the Canary Islands, Manolo Blahnik. With his poetic and ingenious touch he revolutionized its very essence, making it a true work of art. The son of a Spanish mother and Czech father, he grew up on a banana plantation. At an early age he was fascinated by the local craftsmen who made the typical espadrilles, as well as by the haute couture creations he saw in the fashion magazines his mother read. His family wanted him to embark on a diplomatic career, but he decided to devote himself to art. He studied literature and architecture in Geneva and then art

214 and 215 Manolo Blanhik reinvented the heel in the mid-1970s, combining painstaking craftsmanship and unbridled imagination.

at the École des Beaux Arts in Paris. He seemed destined to become a set designer but, thanks to a common friend, Paloma Picasso, he met Diane Vreeland, the legendary editor of Vogue America, who, after looking at some of his sketches, earnestly encouraged him to cultivate his passion for footwear. Vreeland never made a mistake, so imagine if she had made one about a talent such as Blahnik. Manolo began to create his shoes at exactly the time that the most intransigent exponents of the feminist movement began their fight against high heels, which they viewed as a stereotypical symbol of women's submission to male domination. Some extremists may not have liked his shoes, but the rest of the female universe did, that's for sure. As Vogue UK editor, Alexandra Shulman, once said: "If God had wanted us to walk on flat shoes He would not have invented Manolo Blahnik."

Thanks to his skill and inventiveness, and to a bit of luck, Manolo divested the stiletto of its most blatantly erotic quality and clothed it in poetry. And in magic, as Franca Sozzani suggests, calling him, with the utmost pithiness, a "shoe-boots-mules-sandals-magic-maker." He studied art history and the great female personalities of the past and, drawing inspiration from them, he created sandals and toe cleavage that seem to have emerged from a fairy tale, sliding down to us on a rainbow of fantasy. Crystal, feathers, flakes, pearls, paillettes, chains, lace, coral, cherries, and raspberries made of enamel and beads: imagination is the only limit that Blahnik sets for himself in his approach to the redefinition of this heel. His method is that of the artisan, almost of that of a Renaissance master. He works by himself, first taking a few seconds to sketch an idea, creating dynamic colored drawings that are minor masterpieces, then he makes wooden prototypes of his designs, after which he supervises each of the various manufacturing phases. A sworn enemy of the wedge heel, he dwells on the subject of heels: "Even if it's twelve centimeters high it still has to feel secure–and that's a question of balance. That's why I carve each heel personally myself–on the machine and then by hand with a chisel and file, until it's exactly right." Anna Wintour compared him to Gepetto, Pinocchio's "father." And this comparison would be valid if it were not for the fact that not all women are ready to fall at Pinocchio's feet, while they all do so when they see a pair of Manolo shoes, especially leading stars over the last 40 years. Bianca Jagger wore his shoes in her epic-making entrance to Studio 54 while riding a white horse, and Diana, Princess of Wales also wore them in 1994 together with Christina Stambolian's strapless dress, just at the time when her husband publicly admitted that he had been unfaithful to her and when she was more beautiful than ever. Blahnik's faithful include Lauren Bacall, Marisa Berenson, Jane Birkin, Charlotte Rampling, Kylie Minogue, and Madonna who stated: "Manolo shoes are as good as sex... and they last longer." And the list goes on.

From Sarah Jessica Parker to her TV alter ego Carrie Bradshaw. The former candidly declared that she could run in a marathon in a pair of Manolo Blahnik high heels. She also stated she could go into the street

Thanks to his inventiveness and luck, Blahnik divested the stiletto of its blatantly erotic quality and clothed it with poetry.

218-219 and 220-221 The plant world and the various interpretations of leaf, flower, and fruit motifs are among the major sources of inspiration for Blahnik's bizarre creations, so splendidly represented in this designer's colored sketches.

MANOLO BLAHNIK

MANOLO BLAHNIK®

AUTHORS

VALERIA MANFERTO DE FABIANIS, was born in Vercelli. After graduating from a classical high school she earned her degree in philosophy at the Sacred Heart Catholic University in Milan. A travel and nature buff, she has collaborated in the production of TV documentaries and various news reports for leading Italian specialist periodicals. As an expert in photograph editing and the creation of images, she has also edited many books on photography. In 1984, together with Marcello Bertinetti, she founded the publishing firm Edizioni White Star, becoming its editorial director. Among her publications, mention should be made of the successful CubeBook series, *Fidel Castro - El Líder Máximo: A Life in Pictures*; *John Lennon - In His Life*; *Fur and Feathers... ...An Unusual Farm*; *Lingerie*; *A Matter of Style - Intimate Portraits of 10 Women Who Changed Fashion*; *Rolling Stones. 50 Years of Rock*; *Keith Richards*; *Mick Jagger*. She has also conceived and mounted photographic exhibitions that enjoyed a great deal of success in various cities and foreign capitals.

FEDERICO ROCCA was born in Sondrio in 1975. He earned a degree in History of Italian Cinema at the DAMS (Dept. of Visual Art, Cinema, Music and Theater) of the University of Bologna with a thesis on Peter Del Monte, which was commended at the Sacchi Prize competition. He then worked in the cinema department of the Telepiù and Sky television companies, later concentrating on fashion. As an editor and author he has produced *Embroidery – Italian Fashion* (2006), *Silvana Mangano* (2008), *Contemporary Indian Fashion* (2009) and *Hermès, l'avventura del lusso* (2011). A professional journalist, he is presently fashion editor of www.style.it, a Condé Nast fashion portal.

ALBERTA FERRETTI is synonymous with style, femininity, elegance and sensuality.
Her story began at a very early age, when her passion for fashion, which had developed in her mother's dressmaker's shop and studio, led her to open her first boutique in her hometown, Cattolica, when she was only 18. This was the beginning of a successful career. In 1980, she founded the company, which she still jointly leads, with her brother Massimo, and later made her official debut on the Milanese runways.
Success earned her recognition and many awards, including, in 2000, an honorary degree in Cultural Legacy Conservation, for having restored Castello di Montegridolfo and, later, the title of Cavaliere del Lavoro for her service to industry.
The rapid growth in the international popularity of her creations–coordinated by showrooms in Milan, Paris, New York and Tokyo–led to the opening of many single-label boutiques in the world's style capitals.
Energy, charm and dedication are the qualities that have always distinguished Alberta Ferretti, an interpreter of women's desire for beauty, fascination and personality, whose greatest inspiration has been made manifest in such special projects as the *Forever* line–entirely given over to brides–and the *Demi Couture* collection, linked to the charitable Jordan River Foundation headed by Queen Rania of Jordan.
There is a continuous exchange between the fashion designer and women–be they models, celebrities or socially committed friends–who are often protagonists of her show-events and ambassadors of Alberta Ferretti's recherché glamor on the most photographed red carpets in the world.

THE PUBLISHER WOULD LIKE TO THANK THE FOLLOWING PERSONS AND FIRMS FOR THEIR KIND ASSISTANCE:

Alberta Ferretti, Levi's, Burberry, Borsalino, Lacoste, Hermès, Museo Salvatore Ferragamo, Maison Repetto, Moncler, Luxottica Group S.p.A., Gucci, for the chapter 2.55 Chanel, Mania Vintage (www.maniavintage.it - Via F.lli Bronzetti, 11 Milano), Paola Saltari, Parini Associati, Avenue PR and Studio Next.

PHOTO CREDITS

COVER

Grace Kelly and Prince Ranieri of Monaco in January 1956: the couple is immortalized on the day they officially announced their engagement.
© *Howard Sochurek/Time & Life Pictures/ Getty Images*

WS Edizioni White Star® is a registered trademark
property of De Agostini Libri S.p.A.

© 2013 De Agostini Libri S.p.A.
Via G. da Verrazano, 15
28100 Novara, Italy
www.whitestar.it - www.deagostini.it

Translation: Richard Pierce

ISBN 978-88-544-0650-6
1 2 3 4 5 6   17 16 15 14 13

Printed in China